# Incremental Improvements:
## Change Your Life One Small Step At A Time

To Jeremy,

Always keep improving!

*Mike Brodsky*

Mike Brodsky

ISBN: 1503254534
ISBN-13: 978-1503254534

For Lisa, Sara, and Jake

# CONTENTS

# ACKNOWLEDGMENTS

Thank you to my wife, Lisa, for helping me to edit and improve this book, but, more importantly, for her love, support, and total awesomeness.

Thank you to my family for their ongoing support, and for providing me with the life lessons I've learned, which I've been able to share in this book.

Thank you to Alex Tibio for designing the cover, and thank you to Faith Walker for shooting my photo for this book.

# ABOUT THE AUTHOR

Michael Brodsky is a financial advisor in Orlando, Florida. Mike graduated with an Economics degree from Yale University in 1990, and an M.B.A. from Duke University in 1992. He started in the financial services industry with Smith Barney in 1997. Mike has received the certifications of Accredited Portfolio Management Advisor$^{SM}$ and Chartered Retirement Planning Counselor$^{SM}$ from the College for Financial Planning. He has also previously worked as a television news producer with the NBC affiliate out of West Palm Beach, and as a producer for America's Health Network. He is currently the President of the Yale Alumni Association of Central Florida and the All-Ivy Club of Central Florida. He is also a member of the Board of Directors for Distinguished Young Women of Florida, and has previously served as a board member for the JCC of Greater Orlando, the Center for Memory Disorders, and the Orlando International Fringe Festival.

# 1 PROLOGUE

Have you already achieved everything you want to achieve in life? If so, you can put this book down now. If you're still reading, chances are you're thinking about the many things you'd like to change about your own life. We all know what we'd like to change. The question is, "what are we doing about it?" I've met lots of people who seem resigned to accept their lot in life. Many people have adopted a passive acceptance of their current situation, as it would be too difficult to make their dreams come true.

And once we start to look beyond our own lives, we seem to live in a world that's in a constant state of chaos and crisis, at least if you listen to the media's portrayal of it. There always seems to be some major dilemma which threatens our sense of security (September 11 terrorist attack, Columbine and Sandy Hook school shootings, Oklahoma City and Boston Marathon bombings), our global economy (subprime lending crisis, tech stock meltdown, government bailouts), or our health and well-being (killer bees, mad cow disease, flesh-eating bacteria). Each crisis is portrayed as a never before seen situation, threatening to destroy our lives and society as we know it. Those who survived the Cuban Missile Crisis, any major health epidemic, or any major war will tell you stories of the fear they endured, not knowing if they would make it through the challenge. Fortunately, against seemingly impossible odds, society in general in every case survived. Now, I don't want to minimize these threats, as some people did, in fact, lose their lives, lose their homes, or lose beloved family members as a result of those various crises. The threats were real, and perhaps some level of vigilance was warranted. But it seems too many people take these threats a bit too seriously, letting their fears impact their daily lives, disrupting their sleep, occupying their waking thoughts, or perhaps even paralyzing them to the point of becoming unable to function normally. Somehow, some way, society as a whole has managed to survive these crises and threats. Despite fears of global economic collapse, our economy endures. Despite various epidemics, scientists have found ways to control the spread of disease through medications, vaccinations, or simple quarantines. Despite concerns about governmental rivalries which could escalate to nuclear annihilation, we're still here.

Every day, we're faced with a choice: we can live our lives in fear and dread of what is to come, or we can live our lives with a sense of hope and optimism for a brighter tomorrow. But, beyond that, we are also faced with another choice: will we sit back and let life happen to us, or will we take action to influence the outcomes we experience in our lives? Some people may feel a bit overwhelmed by the shortcomings they sense in their lives. It can seem so daunting to ever hope of achieving those seemingly unattainable goals, that it seems easier to do nothing, and to accept things as they are. But what if we could just do something... even a very small something... to make our lives just a little bit better. With that thought comes the concept of incremental improvements. What can I do today to make my life a little bit better? What can I do to make someone else's life a little bit better? What can I do to make the world a little bit better? We're not talking about major, long-term goals; we're talking about small, almost imperceptible changes. But the cumulative effect of these changes can often result in major improvements over a longer period of time. In the chapters that follow, we'll take a look at some of the changes that you can make in your own life. Some of these changes have already been implemented in the lives of others, while some are just concepts waiting to be tested. The best part of this book is its universal nature, as there are no limits to the number of incremental improvements that can be implemented. To reach the author with your questions or comments, please be sure to e-mail mike@incrementalimprovements.com.

We are all imperfect beings. Some people have bad habits... they smoke, or drink, or do drugs. Some people exhibit bad behavior... they're rude, or they're annoying, or perhaps they're abusive to spouses, children, or pets. If one person is able to change his or her behavior for the better, that can have a small, subtle impact on the world, because we're all interconnected. If a thousand people are able to improve their behavior, that's a more meaningful impact on the world. But if a million people all made a concerted effort to be nicer to each other and to take better care of themselves, wouldn't that be something? That's the premise behind this book. Individually, we can each play a small role in improving the world, one small step at a time.

# 2 THE MYTH OF SELF-IMPROVEMENT

We live in a society where everyone yearns for instant gratification. "Get rich quick!" "Lose twenty pounds in thirty days!" "Learn to speak a foreign language in just ten days!" The biggest problem with most of these kinds of programs is that they often don't result in permanent change. Get-rich-quick schemes generally fall into one of two categories: 1) investment strategies which involve great risk, or, 2) outright scams. If weight loss is contingent on following some kind of special diet, or the use of any drugs, supplements, or substances, the results may be difficult to sustain. While it may be possible to learn the basics of a language in a short time period, true fluency would certainly take more time and interaction, to truly learn the subtleties of a language and to converse like a native speaker. Many of us have a hard time adjusting to change. We become used to doing things a certain way, and it's always easiest to go back to our old habits.

So, what does it take to achieve sustainable change in your life? For many people, the pursuit of any long-term goal can seem a bit overwhelming. Experts would advise setting the ultimate goal, and then putting into place a plan of action to achieve that goal. That's all well and good, but how do you begin? My answer is to take "baby steps." You know the old proverb, "A journey of a thousand miles begins with a single step." Let's call this concept "incremental improvements." The idea that if you can make a small (incremental) change (improvement) in any aspect of your life, the subtle change should be so minor as to be almost imperceptible. It should have virtually no immediate impact on your quality of life or comfort level. But once you've made the change, you're ready to make another incremental improvement, just as subtle as the previous one. Adjust to this change, and you're ready for the next step... and so on, and so on. Eventually, you've made a dramatic change in your life, without any major "shocks to the system." Small modifications to your behavior or beliefs are manageable. In other words, these behavioral and belief changes become permanent, because you've hardly noticed the subtle changes in your behavior and beliefs. Your financial plan was part of a well thought out strategy, making small, subtle adjustments to your spending habits and investment activities. Your weight loss program wasn't based on making dramatic changes to your diet or exercise program, and wasn't dependent on any drugs or substances, but was instead based on making minor changes over a longer period of time. And your personal relationships improved just by paying a little more attention to those around you, listening to their stories, smiling a little more when around them, and offering a helping hand when needed.

The concept of incremental improvements is so powerful and has universal applications. It can work in virtually any aspect of your personal or professional life. Want better relationships? Take one step at a time to work towards this goal. Want more customers? Make small changes to your current business strategy, and you'll eventually see the results. Want to be more physically fit? Adjust your exercise program, and watch the transformation occur over time.

We've all heard the expression, "You are what you eat." But it's also true that "You are what you think" and "You are what you do." In other words, changing the way you think (a little bit at a time) can change the way you behave. And, changing the way you behave (a little bit at a time) can result in dramatic changes in your life.

Also, it's been said that actions speak louder than words. Your actions and your behaviors are what matters. What's worse, a preacher who espouses bible verses from the pulpit, but then sexually abuses children behind closed doors, or a loud-mouthed, opinionated person who may occasionally offend others with his frankness, but who volunteers for charity in his spare time, making a tangible difference in the lives of those he touches with his good deeds? Ideally, we should all work to improve our public and private selves, but, ultimately, it is up to each of us to choose to make these improvements.

Throughout this book, I'll share some ideas to get you started on the path to improving the aspects of your life that you want to improve, one step at a time. The great thing about this concept is that there are an infinite number of ways to apply these principles to virtually any aspect of your life. This book is meant to give you some ideas to get started, but it's not intended to be the final word on self-improvement. In fact, you may have ideas that have worked for you… your own "incremental improvements." If you'd like to share the strategies that you found to be successful, please contact me via e-mail at mike@incrementalimprovements.com.

Disclaimer: let's be perfectly upfront here. This book is not intended to replace professional medical advice, so be sure to consult with your doctor if you intend to make any changes to your diet or exercise plans. I've done no research whatsoever into the various topics covered in this book. It's based purely on observations gleaned over the years. Also, many of the topics covered in this book get into areas which might normally be discussed with a psychologist, financial advisor, business consultant, etc. I do not intend to replace these professionals... I just want to help you put things into perspective, and change the way you think about these various issues. I strongly advise that you do consult with an appropriate professional before undergoing any major changes in your life. This book is intended to represent the start of a lifetime discussion regarding ways to improve your life. I hope to keep the dialogue going for many years to come. And, if you have suggestions about ways to improve this book for future editions, or ways to improve the delivery of this message, please contact me by e-mail at mike@incrementalimprovements.com.

# Incremental Improvement Topics

## 3 FINANCIAL

We'd all like more money. No matter what your current financial situation looks like, it seems like there's always room for improvement. There is no shortage of books, magazines, websites, television programs, and so-called experts all touting a wide variety of methods for creating wealth. Many try to promise instant wealth creation techniques. Sadly, there is no such get rich quick scheme... unless your crystal ball clearly shows you tomorrow's winning lottery numbers. Short of buying that winning ticket for a multi-million dollar jackpot, it's important that you first recognize that building wealth is an ongoing, never-ending process which will take you the course of your lifetime. Even after you've reached your initial goal, the wealth building process doesn't end... it just changes a little. You still need to look for tax-efficiency techniques, estate planning strategies, and wealth preservation methods. Whether you're investing your first hundred bucks, or trying to leave behind millions to your family, the investment vehicles people tend to use are often the same. The only difference is in determining the appropriateness of each vehicle for each individual's situation. Hopefully, you've either hired a financial advisor to assist you in this financial planning process, or you've studied this topic closely enough to do it on your own. Either way, there can be room for an incremental improvement to your financial plan.

The first step for any individual investor is to establish a financial plan. Why, you ask? Sure, lots of investors just fly by the seat of their pants, flocking to the hot investment vehicle of the day, perhaps making a bunch of money, and then bailing out just in time, to park some cash in the next "flavor of the month." Sadly, this strategy doesn't seem to work in the long run. I'm not disputing it can work sometimes, or even for a while. But, eventually, the lack of a plan can prove to be the downfall of most investors. Don't believe me? Think back to the late 90's, when the hot topic at every cocktail party was how much money everyone was making in their stock portfolios. And everyone had the same stories to brag about. "Well, my portfolio consists of mostly tech stocks and telecom stocks, with a focus on the dot-coms. And I was up 87% last year." It seemed everybody was making a killing on a bunch of stocks with no profits, but an overly optimistic public seemed all too eager to keep gobbling up shares of those stocks which represented the wave of the future: the internet. A history of those stocks providing earnings didn't seem to matter ... investors wanted to own a piece of the high-tech tomorrow. I think we all remember how that story ended. The damage came quickly. Sure, some investors bailed out at the top, while other naysayers saw it coming and dodged the bullet entirely, but there were plenty of casualties in the investment community, and a whole lot of paper profit vaporized, and the resulting losses were very real and the financial wounds deep. Of course, some investors rode out the choppy markets and recovered years later. But others bailed out completely, with no hope of ever recovering their losses.

Real estate[1] can be a fine investment, as well, but investors in the first several years of the new millennium seemed to forget that even real estate prices can move either up or down. On the one hand, real estate investors don't get the same kind of non-stop feedback that stock investors get. It's not like they can turn on the TV and see a scrolling ticker showing the current price that day for their home, or the houses across the street, updated minute by minute, with experts commenting on the

---

[1] Investments in a narrowly focused sector such as real estate may exhibit higher volatility than investments with broader objectives. An investment in real estate is subject to market risk, economic risk, and mortgage rate risk.

current value of properties (residential and commercial) around the nation. For most real estate investors, the only pricing they're aware of is the price they paid for the property, and the price they ask when it's time to sell their property. Sure, there are some websites that give estimates of real estate prices for your home and those of your neighbors, but those prices don't seem to change very often. (Certainly not every second, like a stock ticker changes.) And, as investors learned by the middle of the first decade of the new millennium, there may be a difference between what they thought their property was worth, and what they were actually able to sell it for.

The bottom line is, each investment needs to be understood for what it is and how it works, and what role it can play in your investment portfolio. It's also important to recognize the old rule you should have heard before, but we'll paraphrase it once again: "Don't put all your eggs in one basket."

Let's get back to the creation of your financial plan. Now, this process is generally best handled by a financial services professional. But, it helps if you at least understand the basic concepts. The first step in the financial planning process is always the identification of some specific goals. A financial plan should never be "I'd like to make as much money as I can as fast as possible." That can be a recipe for disaster. Always identify specifics. For instance, pick goals such as the following: "I'd like to retire at the age of 63, and have $70,000 in annual income available to me, adjusted for inflation." "I'd like to send my 2-year-old son to a top private university in 16 years, and be able to cover his tuition, room, and board." "I'd like to know that if anything happens to me, my family will be left with enough money to maintain their current lifestyle, generating $80,000 per year in income until our children have completed college, at which point, I'd like my wife to still have $50,000 in annual income." "I'd like to be able to afford to put 20% down on a $300,000 home within four years." These are examples of specific goals.

The next step in the planning process is to evaluate where you are financially. And finally, what will it take (annual amounts to invest, rate of return required) in order to achieve your ultimate goals. In other words, how do you "connect the dots" between the present and the future? Most financial services professionals should be able to help you create such a financial plan. And this plan should take into account inflation and taxes (based on reasonable assumptions), and it should also analyze not only what rate of return will get you where you need to be, but also the likelihood that you will achieve your goal.

Once the plan is complete, the secondary step in

the planning process is to design an asset allocation[2] strategy to improve the likelihood that you will achieve your goals. The portfolio of a 60-year-old may look very different from that of a 35-year-old. And, the portfolio of an investor who has an eight percent target rate of return may also look very different from the investor who only needs a more modest five percent target rate of return in order to achieve his or her goals. Make sure to have these plans printed out on paper (not just something you try to keep in your head), as these plans will help to serve as a road map for you going forward. It's important to recognize that this planning process needs to be reviewed and revised on a regular basis.

For some people, it's easy to stick with a plan, and there's enough money to follow through. For others, it's much more difficult, perhaps even seemingly impossible, to save for retirement or any other financial goals. There's barely any money left at the end of the month, so saving falls by the wayside... it can wait until later. And it doesn't matter whether you're making $20,000 or $200,000... if you're currently spending everything you make, it's easy to put off saving, telling yourself, "I'll just wait until I make more money." Sadly, even as you begin to earn more, it will never seem like enough, as there's no shortage of ways to increase your spending. If you find yourself falling into this

---

[2] Asset allocation does not assure a profit or protect against loss in declining markets

latter category, there are some "incremental improvements" you can make which may help you to develop the discipline required to save and invest for your future.

Do you have a budget?  If you've never taken the time to figure out how much money you're currently spending on the various expenses in your life, you may be surprised just how you're spending your hard earned money.  Now, I'm not advising you to live like a pauper, or to give up all of the luxuries you've come to enjoy in your life.  But you may find some of your expenses are unnecessary, superfluous, or just plain wasteful.  So, pull out your checkbook, receipts, and your last few credit card statements and break down all of your expenses by category.  Make sure not to forget any of your cash expenditures (maybe save receipts for cash purchases, just to remind yourself how your cash is getting spent).  List out all of your expenses by category, either on paper or a spreadsheet.  As a starting point, break down your expenses into categories such as utilities, entertainment, food, vacation, education, clothing, rent/mortgage, insurance, etc.  If there are any categories that apply specifically to a hobby, sport, or passion, you can create a separate category for this, too.  Once you've listed out all of your expenses, take a look through and see if you find any expenses that (in hindsight) seem to be a waste.  I think we've all had the experience of looking at something in our home and thinking, "Why did I buy that piece of junk?" These are the items that end up going for pennies on the dollar at your next garage sale. Or food items that you end up throwing away. Or clothes that you're dropping off at the nearest thrift store, after wearing them one time only. These are expenditures that turned out to be poor uses of your money. What if you could identify these wasteful expenses before letting your money leave your wallet? You might notice a common thread in these wasteful expenditures. Do you find yourself buying more clothes than you really need? If so, maybe you need to stop yourself before you walk into the next mall or clothing store. Perhaps look at your closet and see if you really need another outfit or specific clothing item. Do you really need another pair of shoes? Or could you get by with what you've got? Okay, I know some people feel there's no such thing as "enough shoes," so maybe we need to look at other specific items. But the point is, even if you could cut out one superfluous outfit and one pair of shoes each season, that's a decent savings each year, especially over the course of your lifetime.

What about food shopping: do you find yourself buying more food than you and your family can possibly consume? If so, what's causing it? Are your children coercing you into buying items (cereal, baked goods, etc.) that they really want at that moment, even though you know these items aren't necessary? If so, perhaps you need to do your food shopping without your children. Do you find yourself buying more than you need, either out of force of habit, or because you can't remember whether you need another quart of milk or another bunch of bananas? If that's the case, try making a list before you go shopping. This way, you'll only buy the items you really need, and you'll also save yourself additional trips to the store to pick up the items you forgot. Once again, if you can eliminate just one or two redundant purchases, or the purchase of an item that would have just been thrown away, you could potentially save yourself a few bucks each week. Maybe not enough to make you wealthy overnight, but, again, an "incremental improvement" which could save you a decent chunk of change over the course of a lifetime.

Many people have a "stockpile" mentality when it comes to shopping. For instance, "price clubs" are terrific ways to save a few bucks on the items your family uses. One of the catches is that it's often necessary to buy the item in bulk in order to take advantage of the savings. So, let's say you buy the three pack of laundry detergent from the price club, because you'll save a dollar buying in bulk, rather than buying three individual detergent bottles at the store. Is it worth it? Maybe. What we need to really analyze is the cost of carrying "inventory" in your home. I know when I look at my closets and pantries, I see lots of items that we probably won't use or consume until several months from now, if at all. These are items that have some cost associated with them.  Now, it's one thing if these are your "hurricane supplies," or "blizzard supplies," or "emergency supplies," stockpiled for some natural disaster which might keep you isolated from civilization for a period of several days or maybe even weeks.  It's a good idea to keep a stash of batteries, bottled water, non-perishable foods, etc. available in case of some future emergency.  So, these items should be treated differently.  But, if your pantry is loaded with a year's supply of laundry detergent, a two-year supply of soap and shampoo, and toothpaste and shaving cream which you purchased in a previous decade, it's time to analyze and scrutinize your inventory issue.  Many people complain that they don't have enough room for everything.  Yet, many of the items taking up space don't really need to be there.  Also, what is the dollar value of all of these stockpiled items which are taking up space in your home?  Are these unnecessary items worth a total of one hundred dollars?  Two hundred dollars?  Five hundred dollars?  Do the math.  And imagine if instead of having these items sitting on your shelf collecting dust, you had these dollars sitting in an investment account earning interest or dividends.  That's money you could be leaving on the table.  Now there is one other factor to take into account in your analysis.  Some people live very close to retail establishments like grocery stores, department stores, discount stores, price clubs, etc., while other people may have to drive as much as twenty to thirty minutes just to reach civilization. If you live very far from retail stores, then it may make sense to carry a higher level of stockpiled inventories. If you live very close to retail stores, you may not need nearly as much inventory, because it's much easier for you to run out and just pick up a bottle of detergent if you need it. But by keeping the unnecessary inventory out of your home and at the store, you can keep those extra dollars in your accounts earning additional dollars. You can always buy the items you need when you're running low, rather than keeping several on hand for the future.

If some of your other unnecessary expenses are related to shopping, you may need to change your behavior: just stop going into the stores that trigger the buying binges. Or, if you still feel compelled to browse, that's fine. Maybe you need to leave your wallet and credit cards at home to make it a little tougher for you to pick up that next black velvet poster or lava lamp. The bottom line is, the dollars you spend on various products and services are dollars that you'll no longer have for the things that really matter. And these dollars won't be available to earn additional dollars in your investment accounts. Instead, your dollars are now sitting in the product you've bought, which, in most cases, is probably a depreciating asset. Case in point: let's say you're shopping for a big screen TV. With technology these days, you could spend $800 for a pretty nice big screen TV. Or, you could go for something truly state of the art and high tech for nearly $4,000. How important is it to you to have the top of the line TV? Imagine what the extra $3,200 could do in an investment account over a period of several years. You could even take the savings opportunity further, and settle for a slightly smaller TV, perhaps for $500. Or you could opt for an older, smaller TV for $200. Frugality comes in various degrees. And some people are more willing than others to make sacrifices when it comes to material things. For instance, do you drive a $30,000 car, or a $90,000 luxury sedan? You could go for a $150,000 limited edition sports car as a status symbol, or you could save a bundle by opting for a pre-owned vehicle for $8,000. Ultimately, it's your choice. But each choice has its own financial consequences. Saving money is a factor, but practicality, drivability, quality, and future resale value should also factor into your decision.

Need some other ideas for saving money? Here are a few possible ways to save a few bucks by changing your habits and behaviors. Coffee drinkers these days have become conditioned to stand in line and plunk down four bucks (or more) for their super-duper size mochachino decaf lattes. The coffee shops these days are able to charge these high prices by selling the "experience." Now, maybe you've become addicted to the coffee, or the hype, or the ambience, but is the coffee really that different from what you could make either at home, or what you could get from the pot of coffee at the office? Maybe your discriminating palette could never tolerate anything but the four dollar cup of joe, but if you could find a way to brew your own, or find a cheaper alternative (some convenience stores have decent flavored coffees for around a buck a cup), you could save perhaps three bucks a day, just on coffee. What about cigarettes or beer? Later, in the chapter on addiction, I'll talk more about these items, but for right now, let's address the economic factors. Cigarettes and alcohol are heavily taxed items, which makes them prime candidates to save a few bucks, just by cutting back your consumption. If you could cut out one six-pack a week and a pack a day, you might save yourself twenty to forty bucks a week. Dining out is another big expenditure for a lot of folks. Sure, it's convenient, and we wouldn't imagine anyone would be willing to give up this luxury completely. But what if you could replace one meal out with a home cooked meal each week? Depending on the size of your family, you might save twenty bucks (and think of the potential improvement to your diet... see the next chapter). And if you've become used to frequenting some pricier restaurants, maybe there's another restaurant with food you like, but at a lower price point? By replacing one meal at the high priced restaurant with a meal at the slightly cheaper restaurant, perhaps you could save another ten bucks.

Now that we've identified some small ways to

save a few bucks here and there, one "incremental improvement" at a time, the next step is to put this cash to work. These are the dollars you've been used to spending, but what if you instead took these dollars, isolated them out of your spending budget, and put them into some type of investment account for your goals? Which brings us to the next topic, understanding the choices and decisions to be made when it comes to investing.

The first step before implementing any investment strategy is to take a close look at your current financial situation, and see if there are any areas which need to be resolved. For instance, if you're still carrying a balance on a credit card with a double-digit interest rate, you need to get that paid off as soon as possible. There are people out there who owe five thousand dollars on their credit card, with a 14.9% rate of interest, but then they're encouraged by their bank to put two thousand dollars into a Certificate of Deposit (CD) paying 2%. This makes no sense. You could take the money you were going to put into the CD and use it to pay down the credit card balance. By doing so, it's sort of like earning 14.9% on that money, because you don't have to pay that 14.9% rate of interest to the credit card company. Now some might say, "But I need to start saving and investing. Why don't I just keep the credit card balance and save some money for my future?" That's the right sentiment, but you should think it through carefully. Saving money on high interest rate debt is a sure way to save, and it should always beat whatever you might earn on an investment. So pay down those credit cards.

Now, what if you're fortunate enough to have a credit card which has granted you a special, "teaser" rate. For instance, some credit cards will try to win your business by offering zero percent financing on transferred balances, or maybe a really low rate (like 1.9% or something in that ballpark). If you are fortunate to have access to such cheap credit, take advantage of it, and you may not need to pay it off early. But, you need to make sure that you will be able to pay off the balance entirely just before the interest rate jumps. This is a common trap some people fall into. They think the low financing rate will continue forever, but it rarely does. Find out whether the low rate lasts six months, or one year, or perhaps until you miss a payment with another creditor (believe it or not, some credit cards have this loophole built into their fine print). Maybe put some dollars into a bank CD[3] or a bond which pays more than the low financing rate, and which matures

---

[3] CDs are generally FDIC insured up to the applicable limits (currently $250,000). However, the FDIC insurance applies only to the principal investment and will not cover any potential performance. FDIC thresholds are limited to all deposits held in the same insurable capacity at any one issuer. You should monitor, either directly or through an intermediary, the total amount of deposits you hold with any one issuer, in order for you to determine the extent of deposit insurance coverage available to you.

shortly before you'll need the money to pay off the credit card. So, if your investment paid you 3.9%, but the credit card company was only charging 1.9%, you get to pocket the 2% difference. Also, when it comes to credit cards, some charge annual fees, some do not. Find one with no annual fee and you can pocket that savings. Or, some credit cards offer rewards (whether airline miles, free merchandise, or even cash back). A credit card with rewards (all other factors being equal) is going to be better than a card with no rewards.

Also, look at your other debts. For instance, do you have a car loan? What's the rate? Some auto manufacturers are very generous with their financing offers, giving you zero percent, or maybe 2.9% financing, just to get you into a new car. That's a good rate, and you probably won't need to rush to pay down those low interest rate loans. But if the loan rate is higher, then this is a loan that should be paid off, the sooner the better. But you also need to look at your mortgage rate, too. Many people wonder if they should make extra mortgage payments to pay down this debt quicker, or if they should just invest the difference. The answer depends on your interest rate on your mortgage, your ability to deduct the mortgage interest, and the rates of return you could earn on that money at that time. For instance, if you were fortunate enough to lock into a mortgage with a low interest rate (let's say under 5%), that's a pretty good rate. Especially if it's a fixed rate (rather than an adjustable rate mortgage, which might change after a period of time). If bank CDs at the time are only paying 2%, you might think about sending extra dollars to the mortgage company to knock down the balance on your mortgage. But let's say interest rates rise, and you're able to find bank CDs or government bonds (less risky, guaranteed investments) paying 7%. You're better off putting extra dollars towards these types of investments, rather than paying down the mortgage... especially if you're still able to deduct the interest on your mortgage. Why? Because you're borrowing at 5%, and your money is earning 7%, so you get to pocket the 2% difference. If you sent these dollars to the mortgage company, they'll gladly take your money, so they can loan it back out to someone else at a higher rate.

Once you've closely analyzed your debts, also look into whether it makes sense to restructure any of your debts. For instance, if you are carrying some credit card debt with a high rate of interest, perhaps you could investigate whether a home equity line of credit (HELOC) might be a cheaper way to borrow this money. Most banks and other lenders offer HELOCs, a.k.a. "second mortgages," at the "prime rate" (plus or minus 1%). This is probably much lower than what the credit card companies might be charging, and possibly more than what other debt is currently costing you. The bottom line in this analysis is that it's important to closely scrutinize every aspect of your current financial situation to identify areas where it might be possible to make an "incremental improvement."

Another area of your financial situation which requires investigation involves the investment choices available to you. The first question for anyone who's still working is to look into whether your company offers a 401(k), and if so, does your company offer a matching contribution? If the answer is "yes," you need to participate. For instance if your firm offers a "dollar for dollar" match (or even "fifty cents on the dollar") on your 401(k) contribution, you really ought to put enough money into the company's 401(k) plan to take full advantage of the match.

What's a 401(k)? Long story short: it's a retirement investment vehicle, which is designed to encourage you to save for retirement. You'll get a tax deduction on any money going into it and the money grows tax-deferred until you pull it out at retirement, generally after the age of 59½. Please check with your financial advisor for more details about the specifics, including the taxes and penalties for early withdrawals. We also won't get into a lengthy discussion about the Roth 401(k) and how it works, but check with your advisor to see whether this option might make sense for you. Many employees are offered a 401(k), with a very generous match by their companies, and yet they choose to ignore this matching amount. Maybe these people think that Social Security will be enough to live on. Or maybe they think they'll put off saving until some time in the future, at which time they'll miraculously come up with huge chunks of money to save (and make up for lost time). Or maybe they just plan to work forever. But in this era, very few employers offer any kind of pension (except the government and a shrinking group of big companies, often driven by unions). So the burden of saving for retirement really falls on YOU. What are you going to do to save for your retirement? The first step is taking advantage of the 401(k) match. This is one of the few instances where it usually makes sense to invest before paying down even your high interest rate debts.

But, let's assume that you've finally gotten your financial house in order. In other words, the high interest rate debts are paid off, and only the mortgage remains (at a reasonable rate of interest). You're already taking advantage of your company's 401(k) match. What's next? First, go back to your financial plan and review the goals you identified for yourself. Next, prioritize your goals. Then, it's time to begin making "incremental improvements" to move you closer to your goals. If your goal is to purchase a home in the next few years, you'll want to focus your savings on less risky investments like money market accounts, CDs, or government bonds. Stock market investments might not be appropriate for short-term time horizons of less than five years. If your goal is to save for the education of a child, take a look at Coverdell Education Savings Accounts and Section 529 College Savings Accounts. Consult with an advisor for guidance about which types of investments make the most sense in this type of custodial account, but the portfolios you establish for younger children may be more growth oriented (with more exposure to the stock market), while the portfolios you establish for older children should start shifting towards more conservative investments (such as bonds).

If your goal is to save more for your retirement, take a look at making contributions to your Traditional IRA or Roth IRA. (Consult with a tax professional to determine which is better for your situation.) And then invest accordingly in a diversified portfolio that may include stocks, bonds, real estate investment trusts, CDs, commodities or other products that are appropriate for you. And, if you're just getting started with investing, consider mutual funds to implement your investment strategy, in line with your asset allocation strategy. If you're comfortable analyzing investments, you may decide to make your own choices. If you're unsure, find a financial advisor to assist you in designing and implementing your strategy. Don't be afraid to ask questions, and also don't make decisions until you are comfortable that you understand your choices. If you feel intimidated by the advisor, find another one.

If you don't trust the advisor, find another one. If you are unable to get in touch with your advisor when you have questions or need help, find another one. There are plenty of professionals out there, with varying capabilities and concern for your financial well-being, so choose wisely.

If you're looking to become an expert on investing, there are plenty of resources available to learn more about the markets. There are numerous books, magazines, publications, television programs, audiotapes, and seminars all designed to provide information and knowledge about the realm of investing. One thing to keep in mind is that there is no secret formula to achieving wealth. There are no shortcuts. Despite what some unscrupulous individuals might tell you, buying into their secret strategies probably isn't going to make you wealthy overnight. Perhaps the biggest mistake an investor will make is to think that just because they read a book on investing, they're now ready to take on the markets flying solo. Keep in mind, there's no substitute for experience. Don't be afraid to take advantage of the brightest minds on Wall Street, who have devoted years of their lives to studying and implementing investing strategies. Here's the bottom line: Do your homework, have realistic expectations, and stick with your financial plan and investment strategy, even during difficult markets.

This brings us to a very important rule for

investors to follow at all times: *Do not try to time the market.* There will be times when the stock market gets ugly. And you might think the concept of "incremental improvements" would apply here, *but it doesn't.* In other words, just because the stock market took a hit does not mean you should bail out of the market entirely. If your investment strategy tells you to keep a certain percentage of your portfolio invested in the market, *stick with that strategy.* Why? Because history has shown that the stock market will eventually turn around and things will get better. "Oh, but I'll just get back into the stock market when things start to look better." The problem is that no one in the history of investing has ever been able to time the market consistently with any sort of precision, because the stock market is inherently unknowable. You won't know the stock market has turned until after it's already happened, and if you're out of it, you will miss the rebound. "Oh, but I'll get back in when the market starts to rebound." But what happens when the rebound stalls and the market falls again? Keep investing into the stock market, especially during stock market downturns, as long as your investment strategy dictates that you do so. There are always reasons not to invest... wars, assassinations, terrorist attacks, pandemics, and other fears *du jour.* And yet, despite all these challenges, we, as a society, have always survived. People still need to buy products such as food, clothing, and other necessities. People still continue to take vacations, consume energy, and use their smartphones and computers. People will always continue to use the products and services of various businesses, which means that corporate America has always continued to find ways to make a profit, and that's why the stock market has always recovered, eventually. When you own stocks, you're really buying a piece of corporate America. Some people might say, "My portfolio took a huge hit in the last market downturn, and because of that, I had to postpone my retirement." My first question to anyone who makes this sort of statement is always, "Well, why did you have such a large percentage of your portfolio in the stock market if you were so close to retirement?" Anyone within a few years of retirement who is dependent on their portfolio to provide income should start positioning his or her portfolio into more conservative investments. That doesn't mean abandoning the stock market entirely… it just means reducing one's exposure to the stock market. Yes, the stock market may be "risky" in the short run, due to external factors and emotions beyond anyone's control or analysis. But good portfolio managers understand the factors to look for in selecting specific investments, and these portfolios, made up of quality companies, should survive and retain the potential to prosper in the long run. Some people might ask, "But what if the terrorists attack us again? And what if they use nuclear weapons against us? What if our government collapses?" If that happens, I think the value of your portfolio will be the least of your concerns. You can't invest for doomsday. So, let's go with the assumption that society as we know it will continue and thrive. If you disagree, go right ahead and stash some cash under your mattress, put some gold in your safe, stockpile cans of non-perishables, and buy a shotgun to guard your doorstep. Let's hope the world never comes to this apocalyptic end.

The most important thing is to have a plan and stick to it. Your plan is your road map, and while it should be updated periodically, it is never a wise idea to throw out this road map and try "flying by the seat of your pants." It might be tempting to do so, especially during speculative "bubbles," like the dot-com boom of the late 90's. But just remember: bubbles eventually burst. And you probably won't see it coming until it's too late. Instead, work with your financial advisor to structure your overall portfolio in such a way that you have enough cash or "cash-like" investments to weather market storms, so you won't have to sell your longer-term investments, such as stocks, at a time when the stock market is down. Having the proper plan in place gives your overall portfolio time to recover from a bear market downturn, so you shouldn't have to "sell low." Also, your portfolio should be diversified to spread risk so that investments that are struggling may be offset by investments that are doing relatively better. Conversely, there will be times when your stocks are soaring, and you'll be disappointed by the relatively poor returns of some of your other investments. Even though you may want to change your asset allocation to a more aggressive and stock-oriented approach, consider the possible consequences. It is usually best to stick with your original plan, which you designed with your financial advisor, based on your specific goals and objectives, given your personal situation. Don't get too greedy in the bull markets, and don't let yourself become too pessimistic in the bear markets. Stay level-headed at all times, and stick with your financial plan.

This is all well and good for those of you who are already invested in the market. But what if you're new to investing? The first (and the toughest step) is actually getting started. Take the first step of signing up to defer at least a small amount each paycheck into your company's 401(k). Or start to invest that money each month into your Roth IRA. Once you get comfortable with this level of investing, you probably won't even notice this money missing from your budget. So, you're now ready to take the next step of investing a little more. Increase your monthly investment by another twenty-five bucks each month. Wait a little longer, and then bump it by another small amount. You get the picture. Keep making these incremental improvements: looking for ways to trim the excess fat from your budget, and then having the discipline to invest this money for the future. The goal is to continue to contribute and plan for portfolio growth, so you'll have a nest egg to allow you to retire one day.

If you'd like another way to visualize the incremental improvements concept as it applies to financial matters, think about the process of building a snowman. Anyone who's ever built a giant snowman knows it all starts with a tiny little snowball. You start packing a little snow together, roll it around in the snow to grow it a little, and continue the process. It's the same when it comes to money and investing. In the beginning, let's say you start putting some money together to get it into an account that can grow for your retirement. And, let's say you've got $1,000 in the account, and it earns a hypothetical 8% rate of return. Okay, that's a gain of $80. You might look at that and think, that's nice, but it's really hard to get excited about eighty bucks. It might even be tempting to just pull out the money and give up on investing altogether. But think about the process involved in building that snowman. You keep rolling that little snowball around until it starts to grow a little bigger. It's the same with your investment portfolio. So, you decide to stick with it, and keep adding more dollars to it over time, and, eventually, let's say you've got $10,000 in the account, and it earns the same hypothetical 8% rate of return. Now, that's a gain of $800. Okay, that's a little more impressive. So, let's say you continue the process of adding to your investment account until it has grown in value to

$100,000. And you earn the same 8% rate of return, as before. Now we're looking at a gain of $8,000. Not bad. We're starting to hit critical mass. And, just like with your snowman, as that snowball gets bigger and bigger, as you start to roll it around in the snow, it just keeps picking up more and more snow in the process, and that snowball just keeps growing to the point where it's finally big enough to make your snowman. And, in your investment account, let's say you keep up the process until you've reached $1,000,000 in the account, earning the same 8% rate of return. The growth would be $80,000, which is now enough for many people to live on. Whether you're building that giant snowman, or investing to become a millionaire, you have to go through the process of starting with that small snowball first. No one just wakes up one day to find (miraculously) a million bucks in their investment portfolio. It's a long process, of investing a little at a time into investment vehicles that have the potential to get you where you want to go, and letting the power of compounding interest work its magic over a long period of time.

The above example is hypothetical, does not represent any specific investment, nor does it consider market fluctuations, taxes or other fees and expenses that may impact results.

Investment products, including shares of mutual funds, are not federally or FDIC-insured, are not deposits or obligations of, or guaranteed by any financial institution, and involve investment risks including possible loss of principal and fluctuation in value.

Investment decisions should always be made based on an investor's specific financial needs, objectives, goals, time horizon and risk tolerance. Past performance does not guarantee future results.

# 4 DIET

Most people could probably afford to lose a few pounds. Some more than others. If you're in this category, it's also likely that you've tried a diet at some point in the past. There's no shortage of diet plans. Over the years, we've seen all kinds of different diet plans with some very marketable names and concepts. Most advise you to cut out certain types of foods from your diet, or eliminate all carbs, or eliminate all sugar, or eat nothing but one type of food for a week, or drink a special shake, etc. The problem with these types of diets is that they inevitably require you to make a major sacrifice in your life... giving up foods or ingredients that you actually enjoy, and would like to eat. Why make yourself suffer? Why go without the foods you like? What if instead, you could train yourself to just eat less? That's the bottom line, isn't it? If you're carrying extra weight and you don't have a medical condition, it means that somewhere, sometime in your life, you've consumed too many calories.

If you're overweight right now, let's start with the assumption that you're eating too much. Okay, so where do we start? Well, you already know how much you're eating. Let's start with breakfast. Let's say you have a bowl of cereal in the morning. You know which bowl you grab out of the cabinet, and you know that you pour the cereal until you've filled the bowl, or hit some imaginary line in the bowl which tells you to stop pouring, because that's how much cereal you eat. Now, without even getting into a discussion about nutritional information and serving sizes (we'll talk about this later), let's also work with the assumption that your current consumption is too much. (If it weren't, you wouldn't need to lose those extra pounds.) So what if you could train yourself to just pour a little less cereal into that bowl in the morning? Maybe 5% less, to start. Not sure how much that is? Or not sure how to make this change? Next time, just pour your usual amount, then grab a handful of cereal out of the bowl and throw it back in the box. Now you're left with a bowl full of cereal that's just slightly less than your usual serving. Chances are, it's such a small, subtle change, that you'll still be full when you're done. Your body shouldn't miss the extra couple of spoons full of cereal. You've already made an incremental improvement. After a week or two, do the same thing again… reduce your cereal consumption by another 5%. Are you using whole milk? Try 2%. Already using 2% milk? Try 1%, and then try skim milk. Now, some people will say, "I can't get used to the taste of skim milk... it tastes like water." Okay, that's fine. Maybe this is the indulgence you decide to keep in your life. Or maybe you decide that you can train your palette to adjust to the taste, by making incremental improvements. Start by pouring about 5%-10% less than your usual amount of whole milk in your cereal bowl, and then use the 2% milk to replace that missing 5-10%. Chances are, you won't even notice the change in taste. After a few days, replace a little more of the whole milk with 2%. Over a period of a few weeks, you should be at the point where your palette has now adjusted completely to the taste of 2% milk. Next, repeat the process you've just gone through, but this time, you're making the transition from 2% milk to skim milk, using a small amount of skim milk at first, then adding a little more over time until your 2% milk has been replaced completely by skim. This whole process might take several weeks, but in the long run, you've trained your mouth to accept the taste of skim milk, which is inherently better for weight loss than whole. The same concept would apply to virtually any beverage or food (regular vs. low-fat/low-sugar/diet). The low-fat or low-sugar, or better yet no-sugar, version of your favorite foods should always be better for you. *Please note:* This doesn't mean it's "healthy" for you... just better than the regular version of the same food you're already eating. And that's what the concept of "incremental improvement" is all about. We're not asking you to change your life overnight, or making you sacrifice the foods you love to eat. Rather, we're asking you to consider some ways to make small improvements to what you're currently eating. (i.e., slightly smaller portions over a period of time, trying to switch to the low-fat or low-sugar versions of your favorite foods, etc.)

If you like to drink soda, switch to the diet version of your favorites. If you say you just don't like the taste of the diet versions, try the approach discussed above regarding switching from whole milk to skim. (Add a little of the diet version to the regular, and once you adjust to the taste of this hybrid, keep adding a little more over a period of time, until you've trained your palette to accept and enjoy the diet version.) Now, I know plenty of dietitians will argue that many of the diet sodas do include chemicals which are absolutely horrible for people to consume. And it is possible that there may be long-term health repercussions from these diet beverages. But do your own research to determine how the ingredients you're consuming might impact your health in the long run. "Pick your poison," so to speak.

In general, we all know what foods are "good" for us, and what foods are "bad" for us. We know intuitively that deep-fried is always worse than grilled. We know that "sugar-free" or "fat-free" versions of our favorite foods are better than their "regular" counterparts, at least from a weight loss standpoint. (Again, check the specific ingredients of your favorite foods and beverages on a case-by-case basis.)  So, on the one hand, one incremental improvement we can always make in our lives is to identify certain foods which we could substitute in our diets with a "healthier" version. (Even if it's only incrementally healthier.)  We can also look for ways to cut back consumption of the "bad" foods in our diet, without necessarily eliminating them altogether.  I'm sure there are registered dietitians, as well as diet book authors, who are cringing at these suggestions, but the reality is if you've already tried other diet plans, and none of them have worked, then you need another solution.  Lots of people try the latest fad diet plan, and while I don't know the exact statistics, suffice it to say that many people end up gaining back all of the weight they lost, because the changes they've made in their life were temporary and fleeting, and not sustainable in the long run.  If a diet requires you to give up certain foods, your body will probably still crave them, perhaps even more than before.  Psychologically, we often want what we can't have… it's human nature. So, rather than fight your natural tendencies, why not find a solution which works within the general framework of your existing diet, while teaching yourself to make "incremental improvements" over a period of time.

In today's society, fast food restaurants have become a staple of many people's diets. While it would be nice to just be able to give up fast food altogether, the reality is that the convenience factor might make this difficult, if not impossible. However, even the greasiest of fast food restaurants these days is making an effort to offer some healthier suggestions. Most now offer salads, grilled chicken sandwiches, fruit, or baked potatoes. So, if you're used to buying French fries, try one of the healthier sides instead. Or, if you're unwilling to give up the fries altogether, train yourself to eat fewer of them. Instead of the extra-large sizes, get a smaller size. And, once you get used to being filled up by the smaller sizes, start training yourself to get filled up by less than the small order. Take a handful of those fries, and give them away or throw them out. Eat what's left. Over time, the goal is to train yourself to eat slightly less each time, with the ultimate goal of getting the fries out of your diet completely. What you'll probably find is that if you're eating a burger and fries and drink, the fries are purely filler, and you really don't need them in your diet at all. Eventually, if you can order just the burger and beverage, not only will you save yourself those calories and the damage to your health, but you'll also save a buck and change (which you can use to make an incremental improvement to your financial health, as well).

Whatever it is that you've become used to eating,

you already know how much that is. That quantity should become your baseline. Your goal should be to slightly reduce your food intake each day. If it helps, you might want to consider buying smaller bowls, plates, and glasses. This step alone might help to reduce your portion sizes. Or, you can just train yourself to reduce the size of your servings. The most simplistic version of this diet strategy is to teach your body that it can survive on less food than it currently consumes. And by incrementally reducing your food intake a little at a time over a long period of time, you should be able to adjust without any discomfort or hunger. It shouldn't be too tough to cut out fifty or a hundred calories from your diet, and then follow up by cutting another fifty... then another fifty. Your stomach ought to shrink slightly over a long period of time. The pounds should also come off. The weight loss may be slight, at first, but if you stick with this strategy, you'll see the results eventually, and you should attain your ultimate goal of weight loss, but without shocking or depriving your body. Rather, each slight change should be minor enough that you'll adjust without feeling you're missing anything.

When it comes to dieting, experts agree that you should consult with a doctor before starting any diet, and another useful tool is to pay closer attention to what you're consuming by reading and studying the nutrition information listed on everything you buy at the grocery store. Oftentimes, we've become so conditioned to buying certain foods at the grocery store, that we don't even realize just how many calories, or how much fat, or how much sugar can be found in our favorite foods. And we also don't realize what the serving sizes are. Many people who first start paying closer attention to food labels begin to realize that all their lives, they've been used to consuming the equivalent of two to three serving sizes at a time. And they're shocked to calculate that they may be consuming as much as 200% of the recommended daily allowance of certain "bad" ingredients, such as fat, carbohydrates, sugar, sodium, or other substances. If you haven't gone through this exercise, it can be very powerful if you truly want to get a handle on the reasons why your weight has reached the level it has reached. A little knowledge can be very powerful in the pursuit of your weight loss goal. And simply paying closer attention to what your body consumes can dramatically impact the weight loss results you seek. One of the biggest unknowns for most people involves food consumed at your favorite restaurants. If you're not sure about the nutritional content of your favorite restaurant meals, try searching for details on the internet, or find an app which provides this information. You might be surprised at what you find. Now, that doesn't necessarily mean you have to give up restaurants entirely. It just means that you may wish to consider making incremental improvements in your selection of menu items at your favorite restaurants. Or, perhaps finding other restaurants which offer slightly healthier choices. For instance, are your fried food favorites available in a grilled, blackened, or steamed version? Or, if your restaurant offers massive portions, why not just identify how much of the food on your plate represents a reasonable serving size, and then push the rest off to the side of your plate, to be taken home in a "doggie bag." (These leftovers can be consumed as another meal at another time, saving you a few bucks, too.) We've all become trained to eat whatever is on our plate. Most of us have heard the line from either a relative or authority figure to "clean your plate... don't you know there are children starving in (insert name of third world country here)." It takes some mental training to break this habit. Don't let your innate guilt force you to always clean your plate. Maybe you'll feel better sending your leftovers to the starving children of that third world country? Or, just make a donation to charity to rid yourself of any guilty feelings. But it's your health at stake, and it's important to get past the emotions of leaving food on your plate. It's okay to only eat what your body needs. Now, if you're starting to pay closer attention to the nutritional information on food packages, and you're finding that you're still really hungry after consuming the suggested serving sizes, it may very well be that your body is going to need more food, at least for a while. If this is the case, just try the "incremental improvements" strategy of slightly reducing your own portions a little at a time. Once your body adjusts to the slight reduction in food intake, you're ready to reduce your portion sizes a little more. Continue this process until you're eventually consuming a standard serving size, and you should be in great shape by then.

One secret to weight loss is to change your behavior regarding the places you eat. For instance, you probably know that certain restaurants you frequent have menu items which are relatively healthy, while others feature foods that will almost certainly result in weight gain. A perfect example might be the local all-you-can-eat buffet. If possible, try to frequent the restaurants that will be easier for you to "stay in control" when it comes to your eating, and limit the trips to the restaurants which result in the consumption of "heavier" foods or larger quantities. But let's say that you're already at the buffet restaurant. Try to think about what you might normally eat if you were in another restaurant, or dining at home. The goal doesn't have to be to make the restaurant lose money on your meal. It's okay to "only" eat a "normal-sized" meal. For instance, one plate of food at the buffet should be enough. You don't have to go back for seconds or thirds. And go easy at the dessert table.

Which brings us to another little trick that works wonders, especially for anyone with a sweet tooth: teaching yourself a little self-control and discipline when it comes to eating, especially desserts, or anything else that's really bad for you. For instance, let's say you're at a fancy restaurant that's known for their world famous cheesecake. It might be too tough to resist the temptation to indulge, so you go ahead and order a slice. One suggestion: offer to share with others at the table. That will reduce the likelihood that you gobble down the whole, calorie-laden slice. Another suggestion: take a small bite, and perhaps a small second bite, then force yourself to put down the fork and push the plate of cheesecake away. Have you ever noticed, especially when it comes to delectable desserts, that the first bite always tastes the best? That's because it's the initial bite that produces some kind of chemical reaction in the brain, whether it's a rush of endorphins, or just a flood of memories of past experiences indulging in this comfort food. The initial bite is what makes you think, "Oh my god, this is incredible. It's soooooo good." Go ahead and try a second bite. The second bite is pretty good, but never quite the same as the first bite. Try a third bite (if you dare), but you'll soon see it just doesn't compare with bite number one. Why? It's the theory of diminishing marginal returns. In other words, each additional bite will be slightly less enjoyable than the one before. So, if you're looking for a great way to make an incremental improvement in your life, train yourself to only eat the first (and maybe second) bite of that decadent dessert. By doing so, you'll maximize your pleasure and enjoyment of the dessert, while also reducing your caloric intake dramatically, by not consuming the vast majority of the dessert. Just cut out bites numbers three through twenty, and think of how many pounds that might add up to over the rest of your life. (If you need a visual, take the remainder of that cheesecake or other dessert and hold it up against your thigh or belly. Better to leave it on the plate.)

A commercial for a certain potato chip challenges viewers by offering to make a wager regarding your inability to consume only one chip (or trademarked words to that effect). But you can choose to win that bet, and set limits for how much of the "bad" food you consume. When you're at a restaurant, you can pretty much assume that most of the items on the appetizer menu are pretty bad for you, and could be avoided. At most restaurants, the main entrée should be more than enough to satisfy your appetite. The appetizer is often just unnecessary filler, loaded with unnecessary calories. But if you (or those you are dining with) insist on an appetizer, try to opt for one of the healthier menu options. Stay away from any of the deep fried stuff, or anything that's covered in cheese, if possible.

One additional comment to anyone who works in the food service or food production industries: in this day and age of growing health consciousness, it seems there's still much room for improvement when it comes to offering healthier alternatives for your customers. There are plenty of sugar substitutes, fat substitutes, even flavor enhancers (which trick the tongue's taste receptors into tasting something that's not actually there). Why not take the bold step of introducing an incremental improvement to the products you deliver to the grocery stores, or the menu items served in your restaurants, by introducing more items which are specifically designed to be healthier than the "regular" versions? As our nation battles an obesity epidemic, why not be part of the solution, rather than perpetuating the problem? Just think of the increased goodwill towards your company, and the loyalty you'd gain from customers in search of healthier (yet still tasty) options.

# 5 EXERCISE

Exercise, for the non-exerciser, can seem a bit overwhelming. "How do I find the time? How do I begin? I'm so out of shape that it may kill me!" The first step is to make the decision to start exercising. Now I'm not suggesting that you begin by running ten miles a day. You're going to need to start small, making an initial "incremental improvement" to your exercise program. For example, let's say you are a "parking lot circler," always driving around to find the best parking space. Perhaps you could begin your exercise program by taking the spot at the end of the row and walking. You may have only added a hundred extra steps to your routine, but one hundred steps, a couple of times a day, is a beginning. Once you feel comfortable, and you're ready to do a little more, add another element to your workout routine. Maybe you can walk to the mailbox, and then to the end of the street. It only takes an additional couple of minutes a day, and you've already made another incremental improvement to improve your health. Before long, perhaps you'll be ready for another baby step. Maybe you'll do some stretching, or sit-ups, or crunches while watching your favorite TV show. Again, this is another improvement toward bettering your health, and in all likelihood, you haven't really felt any of them all that much. But by just implementing these subtle changes in your behavior, you're starting to work muscles that hadn't been worked before.

There are lots of exercise programs available, including videos featuring all different types of workouts, as well as all sorts of equipment and devices to tone and tighten every inch of your body. And, there's always the gym. Some people spend lots of money on their gym membership, or on buying these tapes and machines for their home, only to see their money go to waste. Now, if you'd really like to get serious about exercise, many of these programs can be a great investment. However, it might not be a bad idea to start small, and work your way up to the gym membership or installing a gym in your home. I've heard too many stories about people stuck with a lengthy gym membership, unable to cancel or get a refund, and too many pieces of workout equipment have turned into very expensive clothing racks. Start with the basics… exercises you know from your childhood. Whether that means sit-ups, crunches, jumping jacks, or push-ups, there's plenty of exercise you can get without investing large sums of money. If you have access to a pool, swimming can be a great form of exercise. So can walking and jogging. Maybe you can join a league to play tennis, softball, ultimate frisbee, touch football, or some other social type of exercise, to make it more fun, and to keep you committed to it. Golf, whether purely social, or for business, can be another way to get some exercise. Especially if you forgo the golf cart, and walk the course instead. The bottom line is, you need to engage in exercising activities that you enjoy, and that will keep you exercising. Now, I would also advise you to consult with a medical professional or an exercise physiologist before undertaking any serious exercise program, just to make sure what you're doing makes sense given your health, and also to make sure you're doing your exercises correctly. But the incremental improvements method shouldn't cause any major shocks to your system, the way a major workout or running program might. Now, you may choose as your ultimate goal that you want to work your way up to the point where you actually run a marathon, or enter a fitness contest. But no one starts an exercise program with a 10K race or a bodybuilding contest.

# 6 BUSINESS MANAGEMENT

Do you hate your job? Ask yourself, is there anything about your job that you like? If the answer is "No," then it may be time to look for another career. But, chances are, there's a reason you're in the job you're in. Hopefully, you chose your career path because of a passion for doing what you do. But not everything in your job is going to be completely perfect all the time. You'll have co-workers you can't stand working with. There are customers who drive you crazy, at times. And there are certain tasks that go along with your job that might be tedious or tiresome. So, what can you do to improve your own job satisfaction? Implement incremental improvements to improve your level of happiness.

A common problem facing people in business is that there's just never enough time to do everything you'd like to do. You're so busy with the various aspects of your business, it seems you can't possibly get everything done that needs to get done. If this is the case for you, you'll need to make a choice: you can either work harder or work smarter. If you're willing to work harder, that will most likely involve working a few extra hours per week. Maybe it means getting up five or ten minutes earlier each day to free up a little extra time, and perhaps staying at work an extra 30 minutes to an hour each day to allow you to get more done. Nothing wrong with this strategy, unless you have a family and loved ones who want to see you and spend time with you. The other option is working smarter, which simply means making incremental improvements to everything you do throughout the course of the day.

The first step in working smarter is analyzing what you do throughout the course of the day. Chances are, you've developed a certain routine. Maybe it starts with a cup of coffee while you check your e-mail. You make some phone calls, have some appointments and meetings, then it's time for lunch. The afternoon brings more e-mail, phone calls, meetings and appointments, broken up with some casual chats with co-workers, an occasional visit from the boss, and a bathroom break or two. Whatever your daily routine, if you want to work smarter, the first step is to identify what you do throughout the course of the day. Write all these tasks down on a piece of paper. Don't leave anything out. If you're in a position which involves a wide variety of responsibilities, keep a running list of all your tasks over a period of several days. If your job is pretty routine (i.e., same tasks every day), you should be able to complete this list the day you decide to start it. Once your list is complete, take the time to really analyze the nature of each and every task on that list. Which tasks are truly critical to your business? Which tasks will put dollars in your pocket? Which tasks are most profitable to you personally? Which tasks are least profitable? Which tasks are necessary, but just don't generate revenues? Which tasks are truly meaningless, and a complete waste of time? Which tasks seem to eat up the most time? In this analysis, start asking yourself a few hard-hitting questions. Look at the business as an outsider, with fresh eyes. Are there any tasks on this list that I could eliminate entirely, without impacting my business? Could I hire someone to perform some of the more tedious and mundane tasks (perhaps even college interns willing to work just for the experience) in order to free myself up to focus on more important tasks that only I can perform? What would happen if I could spend more time focusing on the tasks which generate additional revenues for my business? As an example, imagine you're a doctor. Let's say you're opening a new practice, and you're not sure if you can afford to hire any staff while you're just getting started. So, you decide you can handle the booking of appointments, the billing, the vacuuming, and the appointments with your patients. In the beginning, you might actually be able to handle all these tasks. But, eventually, you're going to develop a practice which serves a growing number of patients. Eventually, you're going to have a tough time answering the ringing phones while you're trying to meet with patients. And at the end of a busy day, you're probably going to be too tired to sit down in front of the computer and do the billing, or to get out the cleaning supplies to scrub the toilets and clean the sinks. In this case, the answer (hopefully) is obvious. You need to start hiring staff to handle the tasks you shouldn't be wasting your time handling. After all those years in medical school, you need to put that specialized knowledge to work by meeting with patient after patient all day long. Your staff can handle the booking of appointments and the billing, and a janitorial service can keep the office clean. You've just freed yourself up to focus exclusively on being a doctor and meeting with patients, because that's what generates revenues for your practice. If you wanted to take your practice to the next level, you might even hire a nurse practitioner or another doctor just out of medical school to help you meet with patients with more simple problems, so you can focus on more complex medical issues. And, as long as the cost of these additional employees is less than the revenues you're able to generate (in other words, it's profitable), it makes sense to keep these other employees. This example might seem fairly obvious, and you might ask how this applies in your own business. But just about every business faces similar issues, which need to be addressed in an analytical manner. What changes can you make, even if they're small, at first, to improve your company's level of success? How can you maximize your value to your company? What is it that you do best that you need to spend more time doing? After implementing the first changes in your organization, repeat this process a few months later, looking for ways to make a few more incremental improvements. This process should be ongoing, throughout the life of your business. Now, if you find you're having a difficult time being objective during this ongoing analytical process, you may wish to hire a business consultant to work with you in analyzing how best to improve your processes, tasks, and systems.

This brings us to the next area where incremental improvements might come into play. What systems have you put into place to make sure that the customer's experience is consistent and repeatable? The larger fast food restaurants are great examples of this. If you walk into your favorite fast food restaurant chain, it doesn't really matter whether you're in your hometown, or on the other side of the world. You know that you'll be able to walk in, plunk down some cash, and get the same meal you're used to getting. Each restaurant might have different employees, from different cultures and backgrounds, speaking different languages, but they all follow the same procedures manual when it comes to cooking the food, adding condiments, wrapping it up, and serving it to you. Does your business do the same thing? What would happen to your business if you weren't there? Would things fall apart? Or would it be business as usual? Some business owners are afraid to take vacations, because they know the minute they leave, it will be complete chaos at the office. What can you do to put in place systems to ensure that the business will continue to function, even if you're not there? You may need to start small and work your way up over a period of time. For starters, do you have a procedures manual? If not, work on this first. Identify the processes that occur on a regular basis. For instance, when a potential customer or client calls in to inquire about your product or service, what do you do? Is there a script that is used to describe your product or service? If not, carefully craft the message you wish to deliver in a script format, and make sure anyone answering the phones has access to the scripts (and, ideally, has committed these scripts to memory). Do you scramble to type up a letter in response, and then start looking for some marketing materials to send? Hopefully, you've already created a kit featuring a cover letter, various professionally crafted marketing materials, and your business card featuring a link to your firm's very impressive website. Don't yet have business cards? Get some. No website? Consider creating one (or better yet, having one created by an expert). No brochures or professional marketing materials? Either put something together, or hire a marketing firm to assist you. Once a prospect becomes a client or customer, what is the next step? How do you deliver your product or service? Do you just "wing it" each time? Or is there a well-defined sequence of events which occurs? Ideally, everyone in your organization is aware of what their roles are, and what needs to happen at every step along the way. If not, start writing down what each person's job entails, including what they do, why they do it, how they do it, when they do it (and for how long). If these jobs and roles aren't in writing, you might think it's unnecessary. After all, "my employees know what they need to do," right? That may be true… but what happens when an employee leaves your business? Sure, you'll be able to replace that employee, but how much time do you want to spend training this newbie on his or her new job responsibilities? And, once the former employee is gone, who is going to train the new employee on how the job gets done? It's much better to have everything in writing, preferably in a comprehensive procedural manual, which can be handed to the new employee, and should serve as a thorough introduction to their new responsibilities. Sure, the new employee will have questions for you, the other co-workers, the managers, and the bosses. But it will certainly save a lot of time compared to the situation where no procedural manual exists.

If you're in sales, or if you own your own

business, or if you're in a position which involves working with customers or clients, chances are you have some customers you love to work with, some you like to work with, and some you just can't stand. Let's face it: everyone has experienced a rude, obnoxious, miserable client or customer at some time in their life. Whether you experienced this individual in your own line of work, or whether you just stood behind such a person at the grocery checkout, we've all seen these negative types in action. And negative people can have a way of really ruining anyone's day. What if we could eliminate these clients from our workday? Can it be done? If it could, just imagine what that might do in terms of improving your own attitude about your work. You wouldn't have to worry about that dreaded call from or visit to that rude, obnoxious, toxic client. Think about how much more positive you'd be about interacting with your "good" clients. And just imagine the impact that could have in terms of the profitability of your business. In 2007, a certain phone company "fired" about one thousand customers who were calling up to two dozen times per month with unusual or impossible requests. Clearly, this company came to the realization that not all customers are worth keeping. Some just need to go elsewhere. Now, I understand that the first reaction most people have when hearing this is, "You must be crazy. I've always been told: 'The customer is always right.' And, if I start turning away business, that's going to reduce my profitability. I can't afford to turn away ANY business." Now, that might be true for perhaps a handful of businesses, but if your business is at least moderately successful, and you have already developed a solid base of clients and customers, imagine if you could get rid of just one customer or client: the worst one you've got. How do you identify this client? It's the one who is the most obnoxious, or the one who eats up way too much of your time asking pointless questions that drive you nuts, while doing a minimal amount of business with you. In other words, by getting rid of this client, you might be sacrificing a small amount of revenues for your company... but just think of the aggravation and headaches you'd avoid by eliminating this person from your business life. And, in doing so, you've just freed up time to spend pursuing another, better, more likable client. Someone you'd really enjoy working with, and maybe someone who can more than replace the revenues you've just lost by eliminating the "bottom of the barrel" client or customer. You've just made an "incremental improvement" to your business. And, imagine if you continued to repeat this process on a regular basis. Always looking to "fire" your worst customer or client, and replace them with another, better client. Eventually, your business would be devoid of all those negative, time-sucking, nasty, low-revenue producing clients, and would be chock full of positive, likable clients, who make your job an absolute joy, because they genuinely appreciate what you do. And what's great about this concept is that it can be applied in virtually any business.

You might ask, "How do I 'fire' a client?" Clearly, you need to be aware of the way in which you do this. If it's handled badly, there could be negative ramifications for the reputation of your business. After all, people may tell a friend about a positive experience with your company. But you can be sure they'll tell *everyone* about a negative experience with your company. (Just check your social media feeds and you'll quickly see what I mean.) So, how do you get the client to leave quietly? Probably the simplest method is through a price increase. Let this client know that you're instituting an increase in price. You can blame it on the increased costs of doing business and providing the level of service you provide your customers. If the client truly values what you do, they might remain a client. If that happens, at least you'll be paid a little more for the trouble and the headaches this client may cause you. If they decide to take their business elsewhere, to someone who is "cheaper," then at least you've accomplished your goal of terminating the relationship. Another effective method is to ask the client for some feedback about the products and services you provide. You can say to the client, "You know, it seems to me you haven't been happy with our products or services for some time now. What is it in particular that we need to improve?" Some times, just opening up a dialogue may reveal a shortcoming in your products or services. And, if that happens, not only might you be able to make an incremental improvement to your company, but you may also end up strengthening the relationship you have with this formerly disgruntled client who now appreciates you more for having taken the time to listen to his or her grievances. And if that happens, it's very possible you've turned a former sourpuss and troublesome client into a devoted fan of your business. Sometimes, rude or difficult people just want to be heard. Give them a chance to voice their opinions, and that may be all you need to win them over and change the very nature of the relationship you have with them. Some people will gripe about the price of your products or services. If this is the only complaint they have, and they keep harping on it, this is someone who clearly doesn't value what you do. This is a client that needs to go as soon as possible. Chances are a price increase will be just the ticket to get the client to take his or her business elsewhere.

Another important task is to identify the relative importance of each client to your business. Does each of your clients receive the same level of service? For some businesses, this is perfectly appropriate. But for other companies, it may be the case that not everyone should receive the same level of service, but should rather receive an "appropriate" level of service. What does this mean, exactly? Well, let's say you've got several messages (phone and e-mail) that you need to return. Which client do you contact first? If you haven't ranked your clients, you might not know how to proceed. But if you have already ranked your clients, you would most certainly return the call or e-mail for the individual who is ranked highest on your list of clients. Also, how often do you follow up with clients? Certainly, the client who is near the top of the list should hear from you more often than the client near the bottom of the list. And, how do you follow up with your clients? The clients at the top of the list might deserve a personal visit. Clients in the middle perhaps get a phone call. And clients at the bottom of the list might only get an e-mail. The point here is that while it's nice to think that you'd like to give everyone the same level of service, this is not always what's best for your business. Not all clients are equal. For instance, if you had two clients who each generated the exact same level of revenues and profits, but one took up twice the amount of time as the other, which client is more valuable to your business? If one client introduced you to three others who later became clients, while the other client hasn't ever mentioned you to anyone else, which client is more valuable, all other things being equal? Revenues and profits are only one factor in this equation. Other factors should include time consumed, introductions to referrals, and likeability. Other factors may come into play, depending on your business. This is a matter that you may want to discuss with a business consultant to determine whether this concept can be implemented in your company.

While evaluating your clients, it's often a good idea to also consult with the other employees to get their feedback about each and every client. You might have a fairly high opinion of a certain client, only to find out that this client is abusive on the phone to your secretary or partner. Or perhaps you were unaware that a certain client was eating up lots of time with demands that your underlings perform various tasks. It is important to listen to the feedback of your fellow co-workers, and to respect their input and insights. No one should have to put up with abusive clients. And, if a client is wasting the time and/or resources of the company, that needs to be a factor in the pricing and level of service for that client.

Now, what if you work for a company or business where you don't have the luxury to select your clientele? You might need to "grin and bear it." And that's not always easy. But you can choose how you react to those negative people. Will you let them get you down? You can train yourself to control your emotional response to these negative influences. Focus on the positive. And this applies to negative co-workers, as well. You may not be able to get rid of negative co-workers (though they might eventually get themselves fired), but you can certainly find ways to cope with their negativity, making sure it doesn't affect your ability to perform your job.

For those in management, or who own their own companies, one of the biggest ongoing challenges is in finding and retaining quality employees. And one of the most gut-wrenching tasks is firing employees for their sub-par performance. As you analyze and evaluate your business, you'll come to find out who your best and worst employees are. The natural question is, "how do you keep your top employees from leaving you to join a competitor?" And, "how do you get your bottom employees to either improve their performance, or find another job?" The answer lies in "incremental improvements."

A top employee is a valuable commodity. The specifics may vary, but the common traits involve some combination of their unique skills, their positive attitude, their attention to detail, their interpersonal skills, their drive and determination, and their unique ability to generate results which boost your company's bottom line. For the bottom employee, the traits commonly include some combination of the following: an indifferent or negative attitude, laziness, poor interpersonal skills, no ambition, and no concern for fellow employees or co-workers. These employees are merely "punching the clock" to collect a paycheck, doing as little as possible to avoid getting fired. But in the process, they may be doing irreparable damage to your business. Clients resent the way they're treated by these employees, and may take their business elsewhere. Co-workers hate having to deal with such incompetence, and might be looking for a way out. On the other hand, a good employee is recognized by clients as well as co-workers. Customers will tell friends and family about a great experience with a company. And employees are often eager to work with certain co-workers who demonstrate certain magnetic qualities. So, what can you do to keep the good employees and get rid of the bad? For your top employees, what are you currently doing to keep them happy? Is there some type of incentive bonus for top-level performance? Money is always a great motivator. And, unless you're living in a Communist country, not all of your employees should be earning the same salary. Are you telling these employees how much you value their hard work? A little praise can go a long way. Are there opportunities for advancement into managerial roles? If not, can you create a new position and title to reward a top employee? If you're not sure whether your top employees are happy, you need to ask. If the answer isn't a resounding "Yes," then you've got some work to do to figure out how to make these employees happier.

What about your worst employees? Are you providing them with some type of training to try to improve their skills? How are you motivating these employees to want to get better? Are they given specific goals to achieve, with a corresponding award? Have you told them what is expected of them in their job? If these bad employees aren't improving, despite your best efforts, it's time to have a conversation. You need to find out if they're happy in their job? What is preventing them from achieving their objectives? Is there any specific training they need, or any specific requests they have which might improve their performance? And, if it seems there is just no hope for turning this employee's performance around, it might be worth encouraging this employee to start seeking employment elsewhere... perhaps with another company that might be a better fit for this employee. And, if the employee doesn't take this hint, or stalls in efforts to find another employer, the last resort may very well be to terminate (fire) this worker. Just make sure you've properly documented all the reasons why firing was the only option.

# 7 CAREER

If you're unhappy with your current career path, it may be time to rethink your direction. Chances are, you can't afford to just quit your job and start looking for another job. But you can take some steps, while still gainfully employed, to begin your search for a new career. A good starting point is to get your resume in order. Especially if it's been a while since you've last updated it. Check the internet or your local bookstore for tips on how to make your resume look as professional as possible, to catch the eye of potential employers. Also, figure out what your strengths and weaknesses are. What skills do you have to offer an employer? You may want to seek out a headhunter to help you in this process of identifying your strengths and potential career paths. A good headhunter can also help put your resume in front of the right employers, and can help you to line up interviews while you're still at your current job. If you prefer to go it alone, you'll need to start identifying potential contacts at other companies, start checking the various job-posting websites, and start sending out resumes. Make sure to use a cell phone or home phone number, and a personal (rather than work related) e-mail address to field potential offers. But what if the offers don't start pouring in? Maybe it's time to make some "incremental improvements" to your skill sets and contacts before pursuing your career search in greater depth.

One possibility is to pursue additional schooling. If you have a high school diploma, consider night classes at the local community college to get your associates' or bachelors' degree. If you're a college grad, maybe you should pursue a masters' degree. If you're looking to make a major change in your career path, perhaps you just need some specialized training in your new field. Check into taking one class, at first, while maintaining your schedule at work. This new knowledge might be just what your next employer was looking for in an employee. And, you've learned a little more than you knew before. As you continue your studies, not only will you continue to gain knowledge which should make you more valuable in the eyes of your current or future employers, but you'll also meet other students and professors, each of whom may have contacts in the field of your interest. Perhaps one of your new contacts will be able to introduce you to a person of influence, ultimately leading to your dream job. It may not happen overnight, but these "incremental improvements" can lead to change over a longer period of time throughout the course of your life. Ongoing education is never a bad idea.

Another great method for finding new career opportunities is through networking with others. If you're looking to remain in the same industry, or if you're looking to move into a new industry, there may be trade groups or associations which you can join to meet other professionals in almost any specific industry. If you're a little more unsure about which specific industry you'd like to get into, try some more general networking through your local chamber of commerce, or other local networking groups. Check your local newspapers, the internet, or even your phone book. Most chambers of commerce will host breakfasts, lunches, or cocktail parties where dozens of people go to meet other business people, in search of potential customers and clients, potential "centers of influence," as well as potential employers, and potential employees. Bring plenty of business cards, and don't be afraid to introduce yourself to others. Exchange cards with those you meet, and follow up to meet for lunch or coffee with those who might be "well-connected." Keep in mind: most people don't respond very well to outright begging, or endless requests for help, without anything in return. So, be aware that if you're able to help introduce others to potential customers or clients (or even potential employers or employees), you might be more likely to get what you seek in return. It's not uncommon to find people at these functions who work for staffing companies or headhunters. Get to know these people, as they will often hear about job openings, and it's nice to have them keeping an eye out for opportunities which might be right for you.

# 8 RELATIONSHIPS

Relationships can sometimes be a challenge. How can we work to improve or better our relationships? We have many different relationships in our lives. There are romantic relationships, whether it's your marriage, or a committed relationship, or just casual dating. There are also familial relationships and the relationships we have with our friends or co-workers. We even have relationships with entities, such as companies with which we do business, religious or charitable organizations, and our *alma maters*. Our relationships may bring us joy and happiness, or they may bring us frustration. Relationships can sometimes be exciting, energizing, and engaging. At other times, our relationships may seem stale, or may seem like they are not providing us much at all.

Let's start with committed romantic relationships. How can you make small improvements which can improve how you feel about, and how you interact with, the person you love the most? Often, especially once you've been in a relationship for some time, you begin to take the other person for granted, or you begin to feel bored or uninspired. If you're looking for ways to improve your relationship, or to bring the spark back, there are plenty of books available that offer lots of suggestions to help spice up, or rekindle the romance in your relationships. But what small things can you do, today, to improve your relationship? One common problem is (once you've been in a relationship for a while) you communicate less with your partner. Or, certainly you communicate about different things. Your communication evolves from "How was your day? Tell me about yourself" to "This is what the kids did… this is what we have coming up… and this is where I need you to be or what I need you to do." Certainly, the conversations can become less mentally or emotionally stimulating once children enter the picture. One small way to bring back the excitement to your communications may be to stop what you're doing when your partner gets home. If your loved one missed the family dinner, pause and sit with your spouse and talk. Not just about the kids. Or, if you've had dinner with the kids, once they are asleep, instead of retreating to separate activities, stop for a minute, turn off the television, and commit to talking for a few minutes about anything, even if it is the mundane. Talk about the things you talked about before the kids came along. Talk about the exciting things that drew the two of you together when you first met. Often, just knowing that you and your partner will devote a few minutes of focused attention on one another will greatly improve your "connection" to each other. Spending time together sends the message, "You are still important to me, and I am committed to you." This small gesture can have a huge effect. In fact, in all likelihood, the time you spend together may stretch from just a few minutes at first, to longer periods of time, and you will continue to feel even more connected to your partner. Not only will you find it easy to devote more time to your loved one, but you'll find yourselves looking for ways to squeeze a little more personal time into your schedule at other times during the week. Just a few minutes of devoted, quality time can have a huge effect, without having a major impact on your "schedule." It's just a matter of setting priorities, and making the time for the most important relationships in your life.

The same approach will also help you to make great improvements in your social relationships as well, or your family relationships. It is amazing to see how much more connected you feel toward another person when you devote just a few minutes to just paying attention to them with no distractions. Put down the cell phone, turn off the TV and computer, and focus. If you find you're having a problem finding the time to do this, take a look at the section on "Time Management," later in this book.

# 9 PARENTING

We all love our children, but let's face it, we all have moments with our children when we may want to crawl under the covers and hide, or perhaps run from the house screaming! Whether it's the frustration from the endless carpooling, or the exhaustion of coming home after a busy day and then having to help with homework, or perhaps the frustration of dealing with bickering between siblings. Our children have obligations, many of which we created on their behalf. Often, we're pulled in two directions. For example, imagine that your children are arguing, and it does not matter whether it's a legitimate argument or a dispute over something petty. Now imagine that your response is to begin screaming back at them, yelling at them to stop yelling. How can you make a small change in your own behavior, to more effectively deal with this situation? Perhaps you could separate the kids, sending them to their rooms for a short period of time, to cool off. Or, you could demand they remain where they are, and not allow them to do anything else until they're able to resolve the situation in an amicable manner, without fighting or arguing. Either way, it helps to speak with them in calm, confident, assertive tones. Screaming at them will only reinforce their bad behavior, showing them that screaming is an acceptable form of communication. If you want to teach your kids to behave in a civil manner with each other and with their friends, it will certainly help greatly if you are able to behave in a civil manner as you interact with your children. It may take some adjustments in the way you've been interacting with your kids, but start by looking for ways you can improve your own behavior, if you want to improve the behavior of your children.

Let's move on to talk about the over-scheduling, and what seems like constant carpooling. Often, the scheduling is beyond our control, left up to coaches, teachers, or perhaps employers. How can we improve this situation, making changes to make things easier, or at least a bit more bearable? Maybe it's as simple as bringing the kids' dinner along for the ride, so that you don't feel the pressure of having to rush the children home and feed them before it's time for their homework and bed? If you could make a sandwich and bring it along, would that make the afternoon a little easier? Then, when the kids return home, there's one less thing that needs to be done. This is an incremental improvement that makes life better in a small way. Also, you may want to invest in a "lap desk" for the kids. That way, while the kids are strapped into their seats in the back of the car, they could be working on their homework. Or, just bring along some of their school books to read during the ride. Think of it as multi-tasking for the whole family. How do you take the various tasks and processes that you normally go through each day, and find ways to either speed up the completion of these tasks, or to tackle multiple tasks at the same time? It's a family affair, so don't be afraid to ask for input and suggestions from the kids about their thoughts. By the way, if your children are telling you that they simply aren't enjoying certain after-school activities or sports, listen to them. If your child keeps telling you how much they hate soccer, or ballroom dancing, or clarinet lessons, then maybe it's time to let that activity go. If nothing else, it will help free up some time. And, more importantly, it will allow your child to explore a new activity, which might be of more interest. Think of it as allowing your child to implement their own "incremental improvement" in their life.

# 10 VOLUNTEERING

Volunteering for something you're passionate about, whether it be as a youth coach, scout leader, office worker/assistant, fundraiser, event planner or anything else, can be one of the most rewarding things we do, as it brings great joy to us in the activity we are physically doing, and also in the satisfaction of knowing we are helping a group fulfill a need that would not be accomplished without us. Now anyone who has volunteered for a favorite non-profit organization knows that what may start out as a labor of love can eventually turn into a dreaded chore, if we feel unsatisfied in what we are doing. If you're no longer inspired, how can you make a small improvement to rekindle your passion for this volunteer activity? The first step is to alert the staff worker for the agency that you are not happy or fulfilled. Most groups want their volunteers to feel as satisfied as possible, as they know that satisfied volunteers are more effective in achieving their mission. The smallest and often most effective change you can make is to let them know that you are not happy, and tell them what sort of things you do like to do. With this simple, small change you can achieve a better result for yourself and the agency. Maybe, after you've made the initial change, you decide you would like to make another small, incremental change in the activities you choose to perform for this non-profit, and that can lead to greater satisfaction for you, and again the agency, and the constituency they serve.

# 11 ADDICTION

Our nation seems to have a huge problem with addiction. Whether it's smoking, drinking, drugs, painkillers, food, or sex, it seems many people have a tough time conquering their addictions, some of which may prove to be fatal. Many will say they're "trying" to quit smoking, or "trying" to stay sober, but they're not succeeding. There is an entire industry devoted to helping end addiction. There are nicotine patches and nicotine gum to help end the smoker's addiction to cigarettes. Heroin addicts are given methadone as a substitute for their usual fix. And "Alcoholics Anonymous" chapters can be found in almost every major city around the country. Many of these programs do work and can be extremely successful for those who get into (and stick with) the programs. Some people try to kick their habits by quitting "cold turkey." Anybody who has been through (or knows someone who has been through) detox knows how difficult and frightening this method can be. It's a pretty major shock to the system. So, let's say you're thinking about trying to conquer your own addiction demons before your loved ones stage an intervention. While you may certainly want to consult an expert on addiction as part of this process, you may also wish to try the "incremental improvements" method.

Let's say you're a smoker, smoking two packs a day. Now, some people who try to quit smoking will substitute chewing gum or eating for smoking. If trying to kick one habit causes another, just be aware of what the new habit could do. (For instance, will you end up with cavities or weight gain from your new habit?) Others try the nicotine patch or nicotine gum, which does get the smoke out of your lungs, but doesn't necessarily reduce your dependence on the drug, nicotine. Chances are, if you're smoking those two packs a day, you've got your smoking schedule down. Your smoke breaks are scheduled on a pretty regular basis, scattered throughout the day, from early in the morning to the time you go to sleep. Your body is used to getting this nicotine fix on a regular basis. What if you were able to cut out just two cigarettes a day? Now, you might have to make some adjustments to your smoking schedule, but would your body really miss two cigarettes out of two packs? Even the heavy smokers we know agree that they wouldn't really miss two cigarettes a day. They may not want to give up smoking cigarettes entirely, but they could handle cutting back a couple. Let's say after a week or two, you decide to cut back two more cigarettes. Again, your body should be able to adjust to this change. Keep it up, and eventually you're down from two packs a day to one. Ideally, you'll stay motivated enough to continue the process. Cut out an extra one or two cigarettes every few days until you're down to half a pack a day. The last few cigarettes may be the toughest, but you just might be able to wean yourself off of cigarettes, assuming you really want to, without shocking your body in any major way, just slowly reducing your dependency on those "cancer sticks." It might be that you never give up smoking entirely, choosing to indulge in one or two cigarettes a day. It's your life and you can choose to live it however you want, and while health professionals would certainly argue that it's horrible to smoke at all, it would seem that getting yourself down from two packs a day to two cigarettes a day is a big improvement. (And just think of the money you'll save!) Ultimately, you'll need to ask yourself whether you really want to kick the habit altogether or just reduce your dependency. If the incremental improvements method alone doesn't eliminate cigarettes entirely from your life, seek professional guidance to take the last couple of steps.

A similar strategy can be used for just about any addiction. If you're a drinker, please think about making at least a few incremental improvements, if not for yourself, at least for the well-being of society as a whole. For instance, if you've ever driven drunk, please take steps to ensure that this never happens again. Find a designated driver, program a taxi service into your cell phone, or just try drinking alone at home. But at least make the incremental improvement to cut out driving while intoxicated, *ever.* But let's say you recognize that you have a drinking problem, and you want to make some incremental improvements to cut back your dependency on alcohol. First, identify the situations in which you tend to drink. Do you drink alone, out of habit? Do you drink in social settings, at bars, on the weekends, with friends or co-workers? How often are you drinking, where are you drinking, and with whom are you drinking? Once you recognize the situational factors which contribute to your drinking, you can start to identify strategies for reducing your alcohol consumption. For instance, if you're drinking a six-pack at every visit to your neighborhood bar, can you cut back to four beers for the night? After a couple of weeks, can you cut back to three? And eventually two? Maybe one? Nervous about what to do while your friends are all busy drinking? Try buying a drink besides your usual beer or cocktail (whether it's a soda, a non-alcoholic beer, or one of those caffeinated concoctions which seem to be gaining in popularity these days). Getting peer pressure from your friends? Maybe it's time to start looking for new friends. If you're "blacking out" on a regular basis from alcohol, or if you find that the incremental improvements method just isn't doing the trick, you may have a more serious problem that requires professional assistance to kick this habit.

Whatever your addiction, the first step is to identify whether your addiction is a habit you really want to kick. If you're addicted to breath mints, for example, this addiction may not be doing any serious harm to your health or the health of anyone else, so feel free to pop another and keep your mouth feeling "minty-fresh." But if your addiction is doing damage to your health or the health of others, it may be worth kicking this habit. Map out a strategy to make "incremental improvements," cutting back your indulgence in this addiction, just a little at first, but slowly, and steadily, reducing your dependence on the addictive substance. If you find yourself going on a "jag" or "bender" after beginning the incremental improvements method, and you find yourself unable to get back on track with your self-guided program, please seek professional counseling to kick your habit. Addiction can be extremely tricky to battle, and while you can certainly conquer any addiction you choose to conquer, it might be easier to have the help of others in your battle. Maybe try to defeat your addiction by teaming up with a friend to kick the habit together, and help provide the moral support to each other to stay on track, or maybe seek professional help from an expert in the field of addiction. And don't give up just because your early efforts fail. Who knows what method will work for you. Maybe hypnosis. Maybe religion. Or, maybe just quitting cold turkey. But it all begins with the first step: choosing to conquer your addiction.

# 12 STRESS MANAGEMENT

It's easy to find yourself getting stressed out from time to time. Different people react to stress in different ways. Some get sick, physically. Some take out their frustration verbally on others. Some cope by eating. The first step is to recognize when you're feeling stressed out, and how you react to stress. If you're not happy with the way you're reacting to your stress, you can change your behavior, as long as you're willing to make this change.

One of the simplest techniques for coping with stress is simple breathing. But not just any breathing. (For instance, heavy panting isn't going to help.) Proper breathing to relieve stress involves breathing in deeply through your nose, letting the air fill up your belly, holding it for a moment, then breathing out through your mouth, your stomach deflating as you exhale. Try this. You might even want to close your eyes and sit down (or even lie down, if possible) while you do this. Think about something relaxing, such as laying on a beach, staring up at the sun, with the sounds of the ocean waves crashing on the beach. Try it again. The more you practice this breathing and relaxing, the easier it should get, until it almost becomes reflexive. If you've just tried this deep breathing, chances are you're feeling pretty relaxed. It's pretty hard to feel stressed out when you're breathing this way. Next time you feel stressed out, try to breathe this way. Once you get used to this breathing and the feelings of relaxation it engenders, you should be able to internalize this sense of peace and calmness, and turn it on whenever you desire.

The next time you find yourself in a situation where you're feeling anxious, or stressed, or even panicked, try to relax, right then and there. Whether it's through the deep breathing, or visualizing something relaxing, or just recalling a sense of peace and calmness, you can change the way you feel. It's better for your health, both physically and mentally, if you can learn to manage and control your stress.

# 13 TIME MANAGEMENT

We'd all like to have more time. It seems there's never enough time to do everything we'd like to do. And, sadly, there is no way to get enough time to do *everything* we want to do, but we can prioritize, and we can look to make "incremental improvements" in the way we use the limited amount of time we have each day.

If you need more time, the first step is to analyze how you're spending your time currently. Chances are, there are certain things you're doing out of force of habit... certain daily rituals that you do every day, but really could be eliminated without having any major impact on your life. Do you find yourself going to either a coffee house or diner for breakfast every morning? Perhaps you could just try making your own breakfast and/or coffee at home, shaving a few minutes off of your morning ritual. Do you hit the snooze button repeatedly each morning before you finally force yourself to get out of bed?

Instead, figure out how much sleep you need each night, and set your alarm clock for the time you need to get up. (If you're still hooked on the snooze alarm, try limiting yourself to one hit only.) That should save a few minutes each day of time that you're just lying in bed, half-awake anyway, lying motionless, doing nothing. Are you addicted to watching too much TV? Sometimes, we watch certain programs simply because we've always watched them. Take time to review what you're watching. Maybe even make a list each week of all the shows you're watching. Total up the number of hours. Imagine if you could just cut out one hour of TV viewing each week. Or maybe even each day. Start by eliminating your least favorite show. And, then your next least favorite. There's nothing wrong with watching good television. But time is too precious to waste it watching bad television.

Also, perhaps you've committed yourself to too many projects, and you feel like you're spreading yourself too thin. Let's say you've got your job (or maybe two jobs), but you're also volunteering for several charitable organizations, taking your kids to their activities, and trying to spend time participating in your favorite hobbies and sports. This is where prioritizing comes into play. Your job pays the bills, so you probably won't be able to cut back the time you devote to your career (nor should you, though there may be room for making incremental improvements to make your time at work as productive and efficient as possible). It's also hard to deprive your children, as their activities are important to their development, so you can't really cut back in this area (though perhaps there are opportunities to carpool with other parents to reduce your time committed to driving to and from the kids' activities.) It's important to be charitable, but this may be an area to save some time. Look at how much time you're devoting to the various charities you feel strongly about, and decide if there are any areas to cut. Perhaps you're volunteering too much of your time on tasks that others can handle. If you have highly specialized talents, perhaps you can make sure that those talents are being put to good use, and you can just say "No" when asked to commit your time to tasks which could be handled by other volunteers. For instance, let's say you're an accountant, so you help the charity with their financial committee, but then they're also recruiting you to volunteer to help sell for a few hours at their bake sale. This would be a great example of a time where it would be perfectly acceptable to ask the charity to try to recruit other volunteers for that task, so you can devote your valuable, and limited, time to tasks which truly utilize your talents. There are plenty of high school teenagers who need to get volunteer experience to pad their resumes as they apply for college. There are also many senior citizens who are retired, and have more time on their hands, to volunteer their services. And, volunteering is a great way for them to stay physically, mentally, and socially active, which can improve the quality of their own lives. It's okay to know where and when to draw the line, and it's okay to decline a request for your time, if you just don't have the time to spare.

Another useful metric is analyzing the value of your time. That is, the monetary value of your time. We all know how much we make when we're working. Whether we're paid by the hour, or paid an annual salary, or work for commissions and bonuses, we know what we make in our jobs. And we also recognize that there are certain jobs we just aren't paid enough to do. For instance, a multi-millionaire isn't going to accept a part-time job flipping burgers for eight bucks an hour. It just wouldn't be a productive or prudent use of time. And yet, when it comes to our free time, we have completely different mindsets about the value of our time. For instance, have you ever been on the phone with a company for twenty minutes to complain and argue about an erroneous charge of two dollars that you demand be credited back? Have you ever driven five minutes down the road (and back) to save four cents per gallon of gasoline to fill up your tank with just over twelve gallons (saving yourself a whopping fifty cents)? Have you ever waited in line for an hour (or more) just to buy a hot new product (such as a video game, or a pair of sneakers, or a cell phone), or to be first in line for a big sale, or to dine at a popular restaurant? Each of these examples listed above represent examples where your time is being assigned a certain value. For instance, if you've spent twenty minutes trying to get back two dollars from a company, that would be an hourly rate of six dollars per hour. If you've spent ten minutes to save fifty cents on gasoline, that's an hourly rate of three dollars per hour. (Way below minimum wage, by the way.) In the case of buying a hot new product, could you have purchased this same product either online, or perhaps waiting a week or two after the initial release, rather than wasting time waiting in line? If you've waited in line for a big sale, how much did you save versus just buying at regular prices? And while the experience of dining at certain restaurants is often well worth the wait, perhaps you could have gone to another restaurant with shorter (or even no) wait times. Not necessarily a direct savings of money, just time. Still, it's an interesting exercise to think about what your time is worth. This is why professional athletes and movie stars earning multi-million dollar salaries will hire chefs, maids, gardeners, and personal assistants to take care of tasks which are not productive uses of their time. But even if you're not a multi-millionaire, you may determine that it's worth hiring someone else to mow your lawn (for example) in order to free up some time to spend with your family. Others may determine that it's more cost effective to just mow their own lawn and do their own gardening, and pocket the money they save. Either choice is fine, as long as you've taken the time to analyze what makes the most sense for you.

Along these same lines, understand the value of your time in the workplace. If you're an attorney, billing your time at two hundred dollars an hour, it makes no sense for you to spend your time stuffing envelopes or filing. These are tasks that could easily be handled by an employee making, say, twelve dollars an hour. This frees you up to maximize your amount of billable hours, while delegating other tasks to another employee responsible for such tasks.

# 14 HEALTH

Would you like to be healthier? Some illnesses are incurable (i.e., AIDS, cancer), though modern medicine is working hard to try to create drugs to improve the quality of life for those with these diseases. Other illnesses can certainly be treated with various pharmaceuticals. Many illnesses can be cured by simply making changes to your lifestyle, such as improving your diet and by exercising. Some have argued that there is even a psychological component to one's health. In other words, a positive mental attitude can go a long way towards fighting illness and staying healthy. That's not to say that a cheery disposition will prevent all illness, but it may reduce the frequency of some maladies, such as headaches, nausea, colds, and more. This very concept may be controversial to some people. Some people refuse to believe that they can fight illness with their mind. But others believe that they can do exactly that. The truth may lie somewhere in the middle, but if you decide you want to improve your health, surely there are some incremental improvements you could make in your life to improve the likelihood that you remain healthy.

Visit the sections on diet and exercise for advice on how to improve your life in these areas. But, surely, research suggests that improved diet and exercise can help to lower blood pressure and cholesterol levels. Diet and exercise correlates with reduced likelihood of diabetes, hypertension, heart attacks, etc. And improving your outlook on life through a more positive mental attitude can also do wonders to help reduce stress levels, while also making you "feel" better. If you're someone who always feels stressed out, be sure to review the section on Stress Management. And, if your disposition and point of view tends to be more cynical and negative, it may be difficult to start thinking positively. But, if you decide to undertake this endeavor, you can train yourself to become more positive, one small mental step at a time. When you catch yourself thinking a negative thought about a situation or another person, stop yourself, and force yourself to think something positive about the same situation or person. Next time you think you feel a negative thought coming on, stop yourself and try to think positively instead. It takes time to change the way you think, but it's not impossible. And you may also need to be patient to notice a difference in your life, but a positive attitude can help make you feel better about yourself and your life, which will also impact your relationships with other people, which can in turn have additional positive impacts on your life and longevity. (Studies have shown that couples in committed relationships and people with multiple friendships tend to live longer lives than those who are anti-social or misanthropic.)

One additional tip for living a healthier life: visit your doctor on a regular basis, just to be sure everything's okay. Regular trips to the doctor can help catch illnesses in their early stages, when they may be easier to treat. If you don't like your doctor, look for another one.

# 15 EDUCATION

Education is an ongoing, lifelong process. Whether you're just entering preschool or a nursing home, there's always plenty more to learn, to enrich your life and sharpen your mind. Some are naturally attracted to the learning process, while others will stubbornly try to minimize the amount of knowledge they acquire. If you're somewhere in the middle, but you're eager to broaden your own base of knowledge, there are plenty of ways to make an "incremental improvement" to better educate yourself. The first step is to determine the subjects that you'd like to study in further detail. Once you've identified what you'd like to learn, you can begin to map out a strategy for your education. Will you use the internet to find the information you seek? Will you read books on this subject? Or, will you enroll in a class at the local community college or learning annex? The correct choice depends on whether you seek to learn on your own, at your own pace, or whether you seek the ability to discuss the material with others.

Another topic of great interest in this day and age is the issue of applying to college or graduate school. It seems to be getting far more competitive to get into the top schools around the country. How can a student stand out from the crowd? Try an "incremental improvements" approach to the application process. The sooner a student begins this process, the better. Colleges and universities are looking for bright students, of course, but they're also looking for people who can contribute in a meaningful way outside of the classroom, as well. So, what is it that makes you unique? What unusual skills and talents would you bring to a school? Find an extracurricular activity that may help to set you apart from the other students. Are you a great athlete, or talented musician, or a dedicated volunteer in your community? Are you a leader in student government, or a member of the debate team, or the star of your school's plays? Find something you enjoy doing, and continue to work to improve your skills in that area, or in those areas. You don't necessarily need to be involved in a large number of extracurricular activities. It can be just as valuable to pick only one extracurricular activity, but to develop your skills to the point where you're one of the best at what you do. Also, when it comes to academics, understand what your strengths are, and focus on highlighting those in your course curriculum and on your application. Always look for ways to improve your grades, and don't be afraid to seek academic help or tutoring to improve your weaknesses. When offered the opportunity to challenge yourself with Advanced Placement or Honors level courses, take those classes! Don't try to just coast through school, but rather challenge yourself academically. On the college board or grad school exams, take some practice tests as early as possible, to identify your strengths and your weaknesses. Consider an exam preparation class, or study some books to prepare for taking the actual entrance exams. On the application, do your best to make sure your essays truly reflect your best work, and highlight your strengths. Start working on your applications early, and try continually to improve your answers and essays right up until the application deadlines. Also, work on improving your interviewing skills, and prepare some stories that will highlight your unique talents, for that college interview. If you really want to impress the interviewer, follow up with a thank you letter, or at least a thank you e-mail, after the interview. You'd be surprised how few students actually take the time to do this. Once you find out which schools have accepted you, investigate the costs of tuition, and seek options for financial aid, scholarships, or student loans. Understand that your education is an investment in your future, and may come with some costs, including your time and your money. But the rewards in the long run are innumerable.

The educational system in this country often comes under scrutiny (especially during political elections as a campaign platform). As everyone questions what we as a nation can do to improve the education our children receive in this country, perhaps it's worth thinking about education from an incremental improvements standpoint. It seems one of the biggest challenges is finding enough quality teachers. As a result, most schools have a wide range of quality in the classroom, ranging from veteran teachers who have parents fighting to get their children into their classrooms, to less talented educators who look at the position as just another job, and who provide little help to those they teach. Sadly, there's not much parents can do to change this situation. Sure, a parent could pull their kids out of public school and send them to private school, but even that's no guarantee that the quality of education will improve... and there's obviously some expense to trying that incremental improvement. Perhaps in this technological era we'll begin to see other improvements in the delivery of education. For instance, we are beginning to see top teachers and professors record their lectures, so that students even in the most remote of areas could see these lectures via DVD or the internet. And, these recorded lectures could be used to help educate other educators, to improve their own delivery of education to their students. Quite simply, we cannot afford to tolerate sub-par delivery of education to any group of students. We need to always keep looking for ways to make small improvements in the way we educate our children. Not just here in this country, but around the world.

# 16 POLITICS

At the risk of generalizing, it seems the reputation of politicians has been steadily deteriorating in recent years. Now, I'm sure there are still plenty of good politicians serving in office. But as the media becomes more zealous in the pursuit of good stories, it seems they're uncovering more and more examples of unscrupulous politicians, exhibiting bad behavior, engaging in backroom dealings, while often putting their own financial enrichment ahead of the well-being of their constituents. Needless to say, this approach can leave a bad taste in our mouths about the profession. Still, the future of our democracy depends on the behaviors of these same politicians during their tenure in office.

Politicians can have a tendency to embrace the party line, sometimes to a fault. At times, it seems they'd rather attack the opposing party, rather than open any lines of dialogue to find any common ground or debate the merits of both parties' viewpoints. But imagine if a politician were to try out the incremental improvement of opening up his or her mind to consider the other party's views. Maybe there are already some of these politicians out there, but it certainly couldn't hurt to have a few more folks open their minds and join the debate for the good of society as a whole, even if it meant deviating from their party's agenda.

And, as tough as it is here in this country to get Republicans and Democrats to agree on anything, it's even tougher when you get politicians from different countries to try to communicate with each other and to reach common ground. Perhaps more politicians will consider changing their attitudes to consider what is best for our world as a whole, rather than just protecting the interests of their own countries. As our world continues to become more globally interconnected, this skill will become more important in the coming years and decades. Let's hope we can all figure out a way to work together in peace and harmony.

# 17 FEARS AND PHOBIAS

A certain talk show once had a woman on the program who was terrified of gnomes, such as the one which appears on a certain travel related website. I don't mean to make light of a person's fears or phobias. I'm sure to her, the fear was very real and extremely terrifying. For most people, the fear of the unknown or the unfamiliar can be unsettling and nerve-wracking. This woman had probably never met a real gnome face to face (then again, who has?). How do you conquer your deepest fears? Perhaps the only way is to conquer the fear head on, but to take it slow, one small step at a time.

One of the most common fears for adults is the fear of public speaking. While some popular television shows have suggested that all you need to do is visualize the audience in their underwear, and *voila*: your fear of public speaking will be magically cured! Anyone who has ever spoken in public knows it's not quite that easy. Perhaps a better solution is to try the "incremental improvements" method. If you'd truly like to conquer your fear of public speaking, start small. Look for opportunities to get up in front of small groups (perhaps at your workplace or in a volunteer organization) and practice short speeches, or just making comments in front of others. At first, even making a brief statement might make you nervous, or anxious, but just start small, and see what happens. Chances are, no one's going to point and laugh at you. Once you're able to experience a little success, you're ready for the next step. Look for other opportunities to speak in public in front of small groups, maybe in your child's classroom, or in a larger meeting setting. If you're still looking to get better, there are organizations around the country which focus specifically on training you to become better at public speaking. Attend a meeting. You'll notice that not everyone is at the same skill level. And the tasks they'll assign to you as a novice won't be too overwhelming. Accept their challenge, and put together a speech for the group's next meeting. Get ready for their feedback, but don't take it personally if they have some constructive criticism. Listen to what they have to say, and try to incorporate their ideas the next time you speak. But if you commit several months to attending these meetings, you'll find each speech becomes a little bit easier. And most people find that after a few months of following the program, their skills have improved to the point where they're ready to face the general public, and even larger audiences. Each speaking experience will give you additional confidence, and you'll learn lessons from each attempt about how to capture the audience's attention, how to speak clearly, concisely, and professionally, and how to better communicate your ideas. If you're able to improve your public speaking skills and master your delivery, the "butterflies" will eventually go away, and fear will no longer be a factor preventing you from speaking in public.

What about a fear of heights? Start by climbing up two or three rungs on a ladder. Then look to climb a flight of stairs and look down. Eventually, you'll work your way up to going up the top of tall buildings and looking over the edge. Eventually, you can conquer this fear, if you take the steps required to do so. Afraid of certain animals (perhaps bugs, spiders, or snakes)? Start by learning more about these animals, perhaps on TV. Then, try to find ways to interact with these animals at a petting zoo or other animal sanctuary of some sort, in a controlled situation. Eventually, you'll become more comfortable with these animals, and while you may not necessarily turn into a fan, you'll develop a level of tolerance for them. Feeling claustrophobic? Maybe try putting yourself into closed spaces for short periods of time, perhaps with other loved ones, or while listening to music, to take your mind off of the situation. You could even try to put yourself into progressively smaller spaces for longer periods of time, eventually without any distractions. Over time, you should have conquered your fear of tight spaces, or at least developed a sense of complacency when faced with that situation.

If you're battling a fear or phobia and the "incremental improvements" method just doesn't seem to be working for you, don't be afraid to seek professional help. There are experts in the field of mental health who can assist you. There is some anecdotal evidence relating to the effectiveness of hypnosis, as well. Don't be afraid to take the small step of looking for a professional, try their advice, and see if it works for you.

# 18 SOCIAL MEDIA

Social media can be a fantastic way to keep people connected. Even though friends and family members may be hundreds or thousands of miles away, you can see pictures of what they're doing, read about changes in their lives, and communicate with them instantly. As technology continues to evolve, there is great potential for social media to continue to play an increasingly important role in our lives. It is interesting to see how people who may be quiet and reserved in person may become vociferous or even hostile or rude through their social media postings on a wide variety of topics. And cyberbullying has already claimed many victims, and may continue to be a growing problem, if we allow this trend to remain unchecked.

So, what incremental improvements can we make to our use of social media, to make it more useful not just for ourselves, but for others, as well? Like anything else, be sure to use social media in moderation. Some people can become too attached to social media, to the detriment of their "real world" lives. Also, I think we all recognize which types of social media postings are of interest or value to us and to others. So, before making your next social media post, ask yourself, "Why am I posting this?" "How will others perceive this post?" Be very aware of what you're posting, as anything posted online will now last forever, thanks to the immortal internet. That picture you may have posted during a drunken moment could come back to haunt you when looking for a job one day in the future. That rude comment or insult, which might have seemed witty at the time you posted it, could end up destroying a friendship, or tarnishing your reputation.

How should social media be used? What is the nature and purpose of social media? This is a subject that will continue to evolve. Some people seem to think it's an opportunity to share pictures of the food they're eating at this moment. Others believe it's for bragging about their children's latest developments and accomplishments. And other people have taken on the role of traditional news media, trying to be the first to get the word out about breaking news or the death of a celebrity before the mainstream news organizations are able to report. There are unlimited ways social media can be used, but we all need to do what we can to make our own incremental improvements to contribute to the evolution of social media. If we think about it objectively and rationally, I would say that "positivity" is generally better than "negativity." Fewer posts are probably better than more. And quality, well-thought out content is always better than a hastily cobbled together reply or random thought.

# 19 ATTACKING A CHALLENGE OR PROBLEM, ONE STEP AT A TIME

It can seem overwhelming at times, to face a particular problem or challenge. For instance, even a joyous occasion such as getting married can cause great anxiety for the bride and groom, and their families, as they try to plan for their wedding. There's so much to think (and worry) about. Who should we invite? Where will the ceremony be held? What about the reception? What food will we serve? What about the flowers? The music? The seating arrangements? Who will we hire as the photographer? The videographer? What will the bridesmaids wear? What kind of wedding dress should we select? How are we going to pay for everything?

Any time you're facing an uphill battle or an overwhelming challenge, regardless of what it is, or how difficult it may seem, nothing is impossible. It just takes some patience, perseverance, and a disciplined approach to dissecting the problem and tackling the tasks, one step at a time. In any difficult situation, first, take a deep breath. Next, break down the problem into each individual task required. Make a list on paper, or a computer, or a smartphone, of all that needs to be done. Prioritize the list of tasks in order of importance. Also, take into account the time required to accomplish each task. Based on the importance of each task and the time required, map out your strategy regarding which task to take on first, second, third, etc. In this way, even the most daunting problems can be broken down and dissected into manageable pieces.

# 20 THE INTERCONNECTEDNESS OF INCREMENTAL IMPROVEMENTS

In the process of making an incremental improvement in one area of your life, it's often the case that this change may end up having an unintended positive effect on other areas of your life. For instance, let's say you choose to give up smoking. The initial impact will be an improvement in your health. But the unintended effect may be that the money you save on cigarettes improves your financial well-being, too. And, perhaps it leads to new opportunities in the relationship department, as you may end up dating someone who only dates non-smokers.

In addition to the improvements in your own life, you may also end up impacting the lives of others you know. For instance, by giving up smoking, you may end up improving the health of other loved ones who previously were exposed to your second-hand smoke. And perhaps your act inspires others to try to make improvements in their own lives.

# 21 INCREMENTAL DIFFERENCES IN THE REAL WORLD

If you're not completely convinced about the power of making incremental improvements, just take a look at the world around you. Think about just about any profession. For instance, the medical profession. Think of someone you consider to be "a good doctor." Now, think of someone you consider to be "a bad doctor." What is it that separates the two? Perhaps it's the reputation of each doctor, or maybe a positive or negative experience you had with each. Maybe the "bad doctor" kept you waiting a long time in the waiting room, or perhaps even missed a diagnosis. Both doctors graduated from medical school, and are probably well educated, with comparable levels of training, and similar levels of experience. But, somewhere along the line, each doctor did something to change your perception of him or her. And, let's face it. Word travels fast. The reputation of a "good doctor" tends to get around. And, so does the reputation of a "bad doctor." Over a period of many years, whom do you think will be more successful? Surely, the "good doctor" will have a much easier time attracting patients, and will be rewarded with higher pay, a better lifestyle, and a stronger reputation in the medical community. The actual difference between the abilities of the two doctors may be incremental on paper, but that small difference can result in big differences financially and socially.

Why is it that plastic surgery has become so popular and prevalent in our society? Everyone looks in the mirror and sees something that could be improved. And it's usually something pretty minor. But millions of people have paid thousands of dollars each to shave a few millimeters off their nose, add a few inches to their bust size, or tighten up their skin via facelift just to appear a few years younger. In more extreme cases, liposuction dramatically reduces the amount of fat in the body, or a few staples are inserted in the stomach to force future weight loss. And while some people may question whether such procedures are medically necessary, most cosmetic surgery patients will agree that the expense was a worthwhile investment. That small, incremental change to their appearance leads to a higher level of self-confidence, which in turn results in improved relationships with others, in some cases leading to new romances or better jobs. At the very least, most patients feel an increased level of satisfaction with their appearance, which has intrinsic value in their perceived self-worth.

Think about professional athletes. Why is it that a top sports star can earn an eight figure salary, while most athletes are never able to get beyond a six figure salary level? It's an example of incremental differences at work. For instance, in baseball, a .300 career hitter gets a hit thirty (30) times for every one hundred (100) times at bat. A .280 hitter gets a hit twenty-eight (28) times for every one hundred (100) times at bat. But compare the contracts for each of these two players. For those extra two hits, the career .300 hitter will have no problem earning an additional several million dollars per season throughout the course of his career. Both players can be considered top-notch athletes, but it's the small, subtle differences in ability that ultimately determine who gets the fat contracts, the endorsement deals, and the admiration of fans.

You've probably noticed this effect in corporate America. Many employees look at their bosses, and think, "I could be doing that. I could be earning that higher salary." And, chances are, they're probably not far off from being right. A little more experience, a little more education, or a little more training, and that job could very well be theirs. There are plenty of stories of corporate executives who have risen from the mailroom to the CEO's office. What's the difference between those in the boardroom and those who clean the boardroom? The differences are probably incremental. The good news is they're not insurmountable. Anyone with the drive and determination to overcome their shortcomings can rise up the ranks. It's just a matter of demonstrating a willingness and ability to continue to make improvements in your life. No one gets promoted from receptionist to Chief Operating Officer without a few stops in between. But it can happen... one small step at a time.

# 22 INCREMENTAL IMPROVEMENTS IN REVERSE

The concept of "incremental improvements" can also work in reverse. Call it incremental regression, incremental deterioration, or incremental damage but it is something we all need to be aware of and watch out for in our own lives. What happens when you have another cookie or piece of cheesecake? Maybe not much, at first, but keep repeating the behavior, and eventually the pounds start piling on. What if you scream at your spouse or kids over a relatively minor issue? You might be forgiven the first couple of times, but before long, even your loved ones might begin to resent what seems to be turning into constant verbal abuse. Companies will often change their policies towards their workers or customers. While the change in policy may initially be perceived as a positive for the bottom line of the company, if the firm continues to make things more difficult and challenging, workers and customers might be turned off, and eventually turn away from the company entirely. This is a theory you don't have to test to know it's true. Chances are you've experienced it in some aspect of your life, and it's never fun when you're the one on the receiving end of this incremental regression. If you find yourself in such a situation, ask yourself if there's some way to turn things around, and make incremental improvements.

Once in a while, we hear stories in the media about a young child who is abducted, and held against their will for years, before they are finally able to escape from their captors. Imagine what that situation must be like: enduring years of psychological and physical abuse with a perception that there is no way out. Imagine the courage it must take to actually attempt an escape. After all, if the escape attempt fails, who knows what further torture the captor will inflict on their victim. But, once in a while, we hear of a victim who takes this very risk to make an incremental improvement in his or her life. This escape sets in motion of series of events which results in the capture of the captor, and the return of the child to the family they haven't seen in months or years. Surely, the victim faces an ongoing period of counseling and therapy to get his or her life back on track towards normalcy, but it all started with the decision to make a change in his or her life. The victim could have remained complacent with the way things were, resigned to the fact that he or she would never get out of that situation. But these brave victims choose to act. Lots of people find themselves in similar situations, some with life or death consequences, others with relatively less serious ramifications, but when you're in any situation which seems desperate to you, you face a difficult decision. Will you grin and bear it, and resign yourself to the situation? Or will you choose to take action to change the very nature of the situation and get out of it? For instance, if you're being abused by a spouse or other loved one, will you stay, hoping things will get better? Or will you take advantage of resources in the community (shelters, police, the legal system) to end the cycle of abuse? If your company is making you work more hours of overtime without pay, or putting you under an abusive manager, or threatening to cut your job, will you stay because you feel no other company would want you? Or do you start seeking another job with another company that might appreciate your talents, or perhaps report this company to the department of labor for workplace violations? If your bank or financial institution starts to impose additional fees on your accounts, or cuts the rate of interest on your savings or money market account, will you stick with them because it's easier to just stay put? Or, do you start shopping around to see if another financial institution might want to earn your business?

An interesting case study in incremental

regression is the field of journalism. Many years ago, journalists had a secret code of ethics to protect the public image of the celebrities, politicians, and sports heroes they wrote about in the paper. For that reason, the general public never read about these icons who were found inebriated, cavorting with mistresses, or exhibiting other deviant behavior. As time went by, though, the news media began to evolve, and not necessarily for the better. Competition to win readers or viewers led journalists to seek out more salacious stories. Before long, it was no big deal to publish a book posthumously exposing a celebrity's proclivity for cross dressing, or other controversial activities. And, as time went by, it became perfectly acceptable, and even expected, to dish the dirt on the living. Today, we find out the names of every performer, athlete, and politician who makes a trip to rehab, or is caught on video in a sex tape, or is accused of boorish behavior. But much of this regression has been driven by the demand for this product. People pay attention to it, and, since newspapers and television networks are paid to get people to view their media, they pander to the basest desires of the masses. In the mid-90's, one local television newscast ran a story about a dog that had been abandoned in a trailer for several days, and the owner was nowhere to be found. The dog looked hungry, and no one could get inside to feed the starving pooch. In another story in the same newscast, viewers learned about the continuing violence in Rwanda, as the Hutu and Tutsi tribes continued to battle, and the mass genocide had resulted in tens of thousands of recent casualties, bringing the estimated death toll to well over half a million people. The video showed the rivers flowing with the bloated, bloodied bodies of the corpses. That local news affiliate received more than one hundred fifty calls during the following day, as the phones were ringing off the hook with viewers wanting to voice their concerns. Every call was about the dog. It seems viewers didn't really seem to mind that thousands were dying every day in a country thousands of miles away. What bothered them was that there was a dog who appeared to be hungry in a trailer somewhere just a few miles from their backyard. Comments varied, but all had similar themes. "They should find the owner of that dog and they should lock him up in a trailer for a week and see how he likes it!" Other callers were less forgiving, requesting punishments ranging from life in prison to the death penalty. I understand the response this story generated... after all, it's a problem which anyone could resolve on their own with a crowbar and a bowl of dog food. Mass genocide is a much tougher problem to fix. Just look at any newspaper today, and it's likely that the genocide in other countries often ends up buried, far behind the celebrity divorce or wedding or adoption of the day. Still, it's also fascinating that people feel a burning desire to comment to their local news stations on the stories of the day. Ask anyone who's ever worked in a newsroom and they'll tell you about some of the crazy calls they've received. And they'll also tell you the names of the regular callers… and the mental illnesses they have diagnosed the callers as having.

It's important to note that while it is very possible to change your own behavior, *you cannot change someone else's behavior* (unless they want to change). You may think (or hope, or pray) that an abusive spouse, friend, or co-worker is going to change, but they won't. You can even rationalize their behavior, telling yourself things aren't so bad, they'll change, things will get better. Others might even promise they're going to change, but unless they've truly bought into the idea of making some specific changes to their behavior, it's just a matter of time before they fall back into the same behavioral patterns as before. For an abuser who is used to resorting to violence to resolve a disagreement, it's probably going to take a great deal of counseling and professional help to truly change their behavior, but an "incremental improvement" might be for the abuser to tell himself that during the next argument, they will only use their voices rather than their hands, fists, or feet. This is an area where professional assistance is not only strongly recommended, but almost absolutely necessary.

# 23 WRAP-UP

If you've made it to the end of this book, congratulations. You've already taken the first step towards improving your life, by reading some ideas about how to do it. Now you need to take the next step: implementing one or more of the ideas. Don't bite off more than you can chew. Pick one "incremental improvement" to work on first. Take some time to get used to this one change, and then you're ready to take on a second improvement. Don't let yourself get overwhelmed by trying to accomplish too much. Also, don't expect to see dramatic changes overnight. But if you stick with the changes, the results will come eventually. Have realistic expectations. This shouldn't be like making a New Year's resolution. The vast majority of New Year's resolutions are broken before Valentine's Day. It's easy to say, "I'd like to lose thirty pounds this year," or "I'm going to make more money this year," or "I'm going to run a marathon before the year is over." There's nothing intrinsically wrong with the sentiments expressed in these sorts of New Year's resolutions, but what's missing is the specific action plans to achieve these lofty goals. And it may seem a bit overwhelming when the results aren't immediately seen. Before long, impatience sets in, and it seems easier to just give up, rather than continue the pursuit of these goals. Instead, make an "Incremental Improvement" resolution today. "I'm going to reduce my consumption of high-sugar, high-fat foods by 10%," "I'm going to start putting 2% of my salary into my 401(k)," or "I'm going to jog around the block every day when I get home from work." These are much easier steps to take, and each represents a "mini-goal," which is achievable and sustainable. And once this "mini-goal" is accomplished, you can build upon it with yet another "incremental improvement" that will then take you one small step closer to the ultimate goal you want to achieve. "I'm going to start ordering 'grilled' foods instead of 'fried,'" "I'm going to stop paying four bucks for coffee, and put those savings into my investment account," or "I'm going to start doing twenty push-ups and twenty sit-ups every day before I get in the shower." Call it a psychological trick, or just a realistic understanding of human behavior, but the premise behind "incremental improvements" is compellingly easy to comprehend, and remarkably powerful in terms of empowering you to improve just about any aspect of your life.

Understand that there is a limited amount of time

and resources to do everything you want to do, so it's important to set priorities, and to be realistic about what you can reasonably handle. With that in mind, ask yourself: What one thing are you going to do today to improve yourself, the life of someone else, or the world? Start with just one incremental improvement, followed by another tomorrow, and another the day after that.

If you'd like to share your own personal "incremental improvements" that you've implemented in your life, along with any of the results you've experienced (so far) or if you'd like some guidance about how to get started, please let me know by e-mailing mike@incrementalimprovements.com. I'd love to hear from you!

# NOTES

# INCREMENTAL IMPROVEMENTS
## TO DO LIST:

1.

2.

3.

4.

5.

6.

7.

8.